OATH OF FEALTY

FEUDAL EUROPE AT WAR

Written by Richard Bodley Scott, assisted by
Nik Gaukroger, James Hamilton, Paul Robinson,
Xavier Codina, David Cáceres, Karsten Loh
and Matt Haywood

OSPREY
PUBLISHING

SLITHERINE

First published in Great Britain in 2009 by Osprey Publishing Ltd.

Osprey Publishing, Midland House, West Way, Botley, Oxford OX2 0PH, UK
443 Park Avenue South, New York, NY 10016, USA
E-mail: info@ospreypublishing.com

Slitherine Software UK Ltd., The White Cottage, 8 West Hill Avenue, Epsom, KT 19 8LE, UK
E-mail: info@slitherine.co.uk

A CIP catalogue record for this book is available from the British Library

ISBN: 978 1 84603 689 7
E-book ISBN: 978 1 84908 086 6

Rules system by Richard Bodley Scott, Simon Hall and Terry Shaw
Page layout and cover concept by Myriam Bell Design, France
Index by Sandra Shotter
Typeset in Joanna Pro and Sleepy Hollow
Cover artwork by Peter Dennis
Photography by Duncan MacFarlane – Wargames Illustrated, Ivan Natario, Frederic Villaescusa & Paul Cummins
All artwork and cartography © Osprey Publishing Ltd
Project management by JD McNeil and Osprey Team
Technical management by Iain McNeil
Originated by PDQ Digital Media Solutions Ltd, UK
Printed in China through Worldprint Ltd

09 10 11 12 13   10 9 8 7 6 5 4 3 2 1

FOR A CATALOGUE OF ALL BOOKS PUBLISHED BY OSPREY MILITARY AND AVIATION
PLEASE CONTACT:

NORTH AMERICA
Osprey Direct, c/o Random House Distribution Center, 400 Hahn Road, Westminster, MD 21157
E-mail: info@ospreydirect.com

ALL OTHER REGIONS
Osprey Direct, The Book Service Ltd, Distribution Centre, Colchester Road,
Frating Green, Colchester, Essex, CO7 7DW
E-mail: customerservice@ospreypublishing.com

FOR DETAILS OF ALL GAMES PUBLISHED BY SLITHERINE SOFTWARE UK LTD
E-mail: info@slitherine.co.uk

Osprey Publishing is supporting the Woodland Trust, the UK's leading woodland
conservation charity, by funding the dedication of trees.

www.ospreypublishing.com
www.slitherine.com

CONTENTS

INTRODUCTION

This army guide covers the armies of Western, Central and North-Eastern Europe in the "Feudal Period" from c.1050 to 1300 AD. The armies of South-Eastern Europe in the same period are covered by Field of Glory Companion 4: *Swords and Scimitars*.

The feudal system, in which a social elite performed military service in return for hereditary grants of land, first evolved in Carolingian France, and gradually spread to the Christian kingdoms of Europe. It never took complete root in the western, northern and eastern fringes. From a ruler's point of view, it was far from satisfactory, feudal service usually only being required for a period of 40 days per annum, though this could be extended in return for pay. This put a severe limitation on the duration and extent of military campaigns, so that often only very limited objectives could be achieved. Moreover, the power of the greater nobles was often excessive, as they could call on the service of their own vassals if they chose to rebel against the king. To counteract these problems, rulers made greater and greater use of mercenaries as the period progressed. These were generally at least as reliable and effective as their feudal counterparts. Money for their employment was raised, amongst other means, by the practice of scutage, in which feudal vassals made money payments in lieu of service. By the end of the period the feudal system was in terminal decline, with most military service, even by feudal vassals, performed on a contractual basis.

This was the heyday of the mounted knight. Armoured from head to toe by the later 12th century, European knights rode heavy horses in tight formation, and delivered a devastating charge with couched lances. By the 13th century horses were also often armoured. Rear ranks were filled by mounted sergeants in somewhat lighter armour. Particularly in Anglo-Norman and German armies in the 11th and 12th centuries, a proportion of the knights sometimes fought dismounted. By contrast French knights were said to be of little value on foot.

Infantry spearmen were relegated to a defensive role, forming up in phalanxes either in front of the bodies of knights and sergeants, behind them, between them or on the flanks. Archers and crossbowmen were usually deployed on the flanks, though they sometimes skirmished ahead of the main battle line.

Major themes of the period include the wars of the Christian kingdoms of Iberia against the Muslims in the south of the peninsula, the struggles of the Kings of France against the Kings of England and the German Emperors, the English wars of conquest or attempted conquest against the Welsh, Scots and Irish, the struggle for hegemony in Italy between Popes, German Emperors and the Kings of Sicily, the Baltic Crusades and the Mongol invasion of Eastern Europe. With dynastic struggles and rebellions by powerful nobles thrown into the mix, Europe was in an almost constant state of war. In conjunction with this army guide, *Field of Glory* allows all these conflicts to be refought on the table-top.

Fully Armoured Knight

FEUDAL CATALAN AND EARLY CROWN OF ARAGON

Catalonia has its origin in the Hispanic March created by Charlemagne as a border region south of the Pyrenees between the Frankish Kingdom and Umayyad Al-Andalus. The Franks conquered Barcelona in 801 and it became the capital of its most important county. After the death of the last Carolingian king in 987, the Count of Barcelona Ramon Borrell did not recognise the new Capetian dynasty and proclaimed independence.

Ramon sacked Cordova in 1010 during the civil war that resulted in the end of the Caliphate and ensured the dominant power of Barcelona over its southern neighbours. In 1070, Ramon Berenguer I purchased the counties of Carcassone and Razés in south-east France, starting a policy of expansion into Languedoc funded by the tribute received from the Muslim Taifa kingdoms. During the last quarter of the 11th century, therefore, Catalonia participated actively in the conflicts between the Taifa kingdoms, trying to protect the interests of its tributary Taifas (Tortosa, Lleida, Dènia) against rival Taifas such as Saragossa and Valencia. The last paid tribute to El Cid in return for protection – he took Count Berenguer Ramon II prisoner on two occasions. Ramon Berenguer III received Provence from his third wife, further reinforcing Catalan influence in south-east France, and led a crusade against Majorca together with Pisan troops.

In 1137, Ramon Berenguer IV was betrothed to Petronila of Aragon, thus uniting dynastically Catalonia and Aragon. Both realms would preserve their laws, institutions and autonomy, remaining legally distinct but federated in a dynastic union under one ruling House. Their combined strength allowed the rapid conquest of Tortosa, Fraga and Lleida, as well as supporting Castile in the conquest of Almeria (1147).

One year after his participation in the Christian victory over the Muwahhidun (Almohades) at the battle of Las Navas de Tolosa, King Pere the Catholic was killed at the battle of Muret in 1213 during the Albigensian Crusade. This marked the end of Catalan influence over Languedoc and thereafter the Crown of Aragon turned its eyes to the south and the sea, with King Jaume I the Conqueror subjugating the kingdoms of Majorca (1229) and Valencia (1238), his son Pere the Great becoming King of Sicily (1282) and defeating the subsequent French invasion of Catalonia (1285), and finally Alfons IV of Aragon (III of Catalonia) consolidating the Mediterranean empire with the invasion of Sardinia (1323) and nominal rule over Athens and Neopatria after they were conquered by the Catalan Company.

This list covers the armies of Catalonia from its independence from Frankish rule in 988, and the armies of the Crown of Aragon from its creation until the accession of Pere IV of Aragon (III of Catalonia) in 1336.

TROOP NOTES

Early armies had a very strong Frankish influence mixed with local developments.

Drilled militia from the cities used pikes from the 13th century, but deep formations were not introduced until the arrival of foreign mercenaries in the second half of the 15th century. Catalan wall paintings of the 13th century appear to show mixed bodies of spearmen and heavier

armoured soldiers with swords, the swordsmen in the front rank and the spearmen behind.

They adopted an aggressive stance in battle – for example, at the battle of Portopi, just after the

army disembarked in Majorca, while the knights were still reluctant to attack the Muslim army, it was the city militia who attacked first, forcing the knights to follow them.

Almughavars were recruited from the border lands and are described as lightly armoured and equipped with a couple of iron darts called sagetes or escones, similar to the Roman pilum or the ancient Spanish soliferrum, a short sword or dagger, and a spear. Their fighting style relied on the effect of missiles combined with a fierce charge. Classification presents a problem – therefore we give a choice.

The military orders in the Iberian Peninsula were more numerous than those of other countries, but their knights were on some occasions less controllable, hence the option to grade them as Undrilled.

A proportion of the army's spearmen, crossbowmen or archers can be Mudejars (Muslims) or Jews conscripted from the formerly Muslim areas. This does not affect their classification.

Military Orders Knight

EARLY CROWN OF ARAGON STARTER ARMY 1276 AD		
Commander-in-Chief	1	Field Commander
Sub-commanders	2	2 x Troop Commander
Feudal knights	2 BGs	Each comprising 4 bases of feudal knights: Superior, Heavily Armoured, Undrilled Knights – Lancers, Swordsmen
Separately deployed cavalls alforrats	1 BG	4 bases of cavalls alforrats: Average, Armoured, Undrilled Cavalry – Lancers, Swordsmen
Jinetes	1 BG	4 bases of jinetes: Average, Unprotected, Undrilled Light Horse – Javelins, Light Spear
Spearmen	2 BGs	Each comprising 6 bases of spearmen: Average, Protected, Undrilled Heavy Foot – Defensive Spearmen
Crossbowmen	1 BG	8 bases of crossbowmen: Average, Unprotected, Undrilled Light Foot – Crossbow
Almughavars	2 BGs	Each comprising 6 bases of almughavars: Superior, Protected, Undrilled Medium Foot – Offensive Spearmen
Camp	1	Unfortified camp
Total	9 BGs	Camp, 16 mounted bases, 32 foot bases, 3 commanders

BUILDING A CUSTOMISED LIST USING OUR ARMY POINTS

Choose an army based on the maxima and minima in the list below. The following special instructions apply to this army:

- Commanders should be depicted as knights.
- The minimum marked * applies only if no almughavars are used.

- The minima marked ** apply if any almughavars or almughavar skirmishers are used.
- Andalusian allies in 1010 cannot include Arab troops.
- All Medium Foot almughavars must be classified the same.

Crossbowman

FEUDAL CATALAN AND EARLY CROWN OF ARAGON

Territory Types: Agricultural, Developed, Hilly

C-in-C	Inspired Commander/Field Commander/Troop Commander					80/50/35	1	
Sub-commanders	Field Commander					50	0–2	
	Troop Commander					35	0–3	

Troop name		Troop Type				Capabilities		Points per base	Bases per BG	Total bases
		Type	Armour	Quality	Training	Shooting	Close Combat			
Core Troops										
Feudal knights	Only before 1050	Cavalry	Armoured	Superior	Undrilled	–	Lancers, Swordsmen	16	4–6	6–36
	Only from 1050 to 1149	Knights	Armoured	Superior	Undrilled	–	Lancers, Swordsmen	20	4–6	6–36
	Only from 1150	Knights	Heavily Armoured	Superior	Undrilled	–	Lancers, Swordsmen	23	4–6	6–24
Spearmen		Heavy Foot	Protected	Average	Undrilled	–	Defensive Spearmen	6	6–8	0–32 *8–36
				Poor				4		
City militia	Only from 1200	Heavy Foot	Protected	Average	Drilled	–	Offensive Spearmen	8	6–8	0–12
Almughavars	Only from 1150	Medium Foot	Unprotected	Superior	Undrilled	–	Offensive Spearmen	7	6–8	**6–32
			Protected					9		
			Unprotected	Superior	Undrilled	–	Impact Foot, Swordsmen	7		
			Protected					9		
Almughavar skirmishers		Light Foot	Unprotected	Average	Undrilled	Javelins	Light Spear	4	4–6	0–6
Crossbowmen	Any date	Medium Foot	Protected	Average	Undrilled	Crossbow	–	6	6–8	Before 1150 0–8, From 1150 8–24
		Light Foot	Unprotected	Average	Undrilled	Crossbow	–	5	6–8	
	Only from 1200	Medium Foot	Protected	Average	Drilled	Crossbow	–	7	6–8	
Optional Troops										
Separately deployed cavalls alforrats	Only from 1275	Cavalry	Armoured	Average	Undrilled	–	Lancers, Swordsmen	12	4–6	0–6
Jinetes	Only from 1200	Light Horse	Unprotected	Average	Undrilled	Javelins	Light Spear	7	4–6	0–6
	Only from 1300	Light Horse	Protected	Average	Undrilled	Javelins	Light Spear	8	4–6	
Mounted crossbowmen	Only from 1150	Light Horse	Unprotected	Average	Undrilled	Crossbow	–	7	4–6	0–6
			Protected					8		
Mercenary Berber light horse		Light Horse	Unprotected	Average	Undrilled	Javelins	Light Spear	7	4–6	0–6

Troop name		Type	Armour	Quality	Training	Shooting	Close Combat	Points per base	Bases per BG	Total bases
Military Orders knights	Only from 1100 to 1149	Knights	Armoured	Superior	Drilled	–	Lancers, Swordsmen	22	4–6	0–8
					Undrilled			20		
	Only from 1150	Knights	Heavily Armoured	Superior	Drilled	–	Lancers, Swordsmen	26	4–6	
					Undrilled			23		
Military order spearmen	Only from 1100	Heavy Foot	Protected	Average	Drilled	–	Defensive Spearmen	7	6–8	0–8
			Armoured					9		
Military order crossbowmen		Medium Foot	Protected	Average	Drilled	Crossbow	–	7	4–6	0–6
Javelinmen	Only before 1150	Medium Foot	Unprotected	Average	Undrilled	–	Light Spear	4	6–8	0–16
			Protected					5		
		Light Foot	Unprotected	Average	Undrilled	Javelins	Light Spear	4		
Archers		Light Foot	Unprotected	Average	Undrilled	Bow	–	5	6–8	0–8
Slingers		Light Foot	Unprotected	Average	Undrilled	Sling	–	4	6–8	0–8
Fortified camp								24		0–1

Allies		
Taifa Andalusian allies (only from 1031 to 1100) – Taifa Andalusian		

Special Campaigns		
Expedition to Cordova in 1010		
Andalusian allies – Andalusian – See Field of Glory Companion 8: *Wolves from the Sea: The Dark Ages*		
Majorca Crusade 1113 to 1115		
Pisan allies – Italian Communal		

FEUDAL CATALAN AND EARLY CROWN OF ARAGON ALLIES

Allied commander			Field Commander/Troop Commander					40/25		1
Troop name		Troop Type				Capabilities		Points per base	Bases per BG	Total bases
		Type	Armour	Quality	Training	Shooting	Close Combat			
Feudal knights	Only before 1050	Cavalry	Armoured	Superior	Undrilled	–	Lancers, Swordsmen	16	4–6	4–8
	Only from 1050 to 1149	Knights	Armoured	Superior	Undrilled	–	Lancers, Swordsmen	20	4–6	
	Only from 1150	Knights	Heavily Armoured	Superior	Undrilled	–	Lancers, Swordsmen	23	4–6	
Spearmen		Heavy Foot	Protected	Average	Undrilled	–	Defensive Spearmen	6	6–8	0–8	*4–12
				Poor				4		
City militia	Only from 1200	Heavy Foot	Protected	Average	Drilled	–	Offensive Spearmen	8	4	0–4
Almughavars	Only from 1150	Medium Foot	Unprotected	Superior	Undrilled	–	Offensive Spearmen	7	6–8	0–8
			Protected					9		
			Unprotected	Superior	Undrilled	–	Impact Foot, Swordsmen	7		
			Protected					9		
Crossbowmen	Only from 1150	Medium Foot	Protected	Average	Undrilled	Crossbow	–	6	6–8	6–8
		Light Foot	Unprotected	Average	Undrilled	Crossbow	–	5	6–8	
	Only from 1200	Medium Foot	Protected	Average	Drilled	Crossbow	–	7	6–8	
Javelinmen	Only before 1150	Medium Foot	Unprotected	Average	Undrilled	–	Light Spear	5	4	0–4
			Protected					4		
		Light Foot	Unprotected	Average	Undrilled	Javelins	Light Spear	4		

Saragossan troops, by Angus McBride. Taken from Men-at-Arms 200: El Cid and the Reconquista 1050–1492

EARLY HUNGARIAN

In 1000 the Magyar High Prince, Vajk, of the Árpád dynasty, accepted Christianity. He was recognised as King of Hungary by Pope Sylvester II and ruled under his Christian name of István (Stephen) I. Under his successors Hungary developed a feudal economy and expanded its territories, becoming one of the leading powers in south-eastern Europe.

Until the 13th century, the Árpád kings enjoyed more or less absolute power. In the early 13th century, however, they found it necessary to make large land grants to the nobles, shifting the balance of power in favour of the magnates. When the Mongols invaded in 1241, many of the magnates failed to answer the call of King Béla IV, who was severely defeated at the Battle of Mohi. The Mongols caused much devastation and slaughtered up to a third of the population before being recalled to elect a new Great Khan on the death of Ögedei in 1242.

The last king of the Árpád line, András III, died in 1301. Following a protracted succession struggle, the Angevin Charles I Robert ascended the throne in 1308. This list covers Hungarian armies from 1000 to 1308.

TROOP NOTES

Though primarily equipped with lance and shield, Hungarian armoured cavalry continued to carry bows and operate as heavy horse archers when necessary until the end of the 12th century.

Many western knights, principally Germans and Italians, were employed as mercenaries and subsequently granted Hungarian lands especially in the east of the kingdom. They gradually became absorbed into the Hungarian nobility,

Italian Knight

who themselves came to adopt their equipment and tactics. The king's household and court were the first to do so.

Classification of Szeklers presents some difficulty, so we have given a choice of interpretations.

Cuman prisoners of war were settled on the frontier from the later 11th century. In 1239, however, 40,000 of them under Khan Kötöny were accepted into Hungary following their defeat by the Mongols, in return for military service. A stormy relationship ensued, with several attempts being made to purge them before they finally agreed at the end of the 13th century to accept Christianity, adopt a settled life style and stop killing Hungarians.

EARLY HUNGARIAN STARTER ARMY 1175 AD		
Commander-in-Chief	1	Field Commander
Sub-commanders	2	2 x Troop Commander
Hungarian nobles and gentry	1 BG	4 bases of Hungarian nobles and gentry: Superior, Heavily Armoured, Undrilled Knights – Lancers, Swordsmen
Hungarian nobles and gentry	2 BGs	Each comprising 4 bases of Hungarian nobles and gentry: Superior, Armoured, Undrilled Cavalry – Bow*, Light Spear, Swordsmen
German knights and sergeants	1 BG	4 bases of German knights and sergeants: Superior, Heavily Armoured, Undrilled Knights – Lancers, Swordsmen
Horse archers	4 BGs	Each comprising 4 bases of horse archers: Average, Unprotected, Undrilled Light Horse – Bow
Foot archers	1 BG	8 bases of foot archers: Poor, Unprotected, Undrilled Light Foot – Bow
Camp	1	Unfortified camp
Total	9 BGs	Camp, 32 mounted bases, 8 foot bases, 3 commanders

BUILDING A CUSTOMISED LIST USING OUR ARMY POINTS

Choose an army based on the maxima and minima in the list below. The following special instructions apply to this army:

- Commanders should be depicted as nobles.
- Only one allied contingent can be used.

Hungarian Archer

EARLY HUNGARIAN

Territory Types: Agricultural, Hilly

C-in-C	Inspired Commander/Field Commander/Troop Commander					80/50/35	1	
Sub-commanders	Field Commander					50	0–2	
	Troop Commander					35	0–3	

Troop name	Troop Type				Capabilities		Points per base	Bases per BG	Total bases
	Type	Armour	Quality	Training	Shooting	Close Combat			
Core Troops									
Hungarian nobles and gentry	Only before 1200	Cavalry	Armoured	Superior	Undrilled	Bow*	Light Spear, Swordsmen	18	4–6	0–8
	Only before 1050	Cavalry	Armoured	Superior	Undrilled	–	Lancers, Swordsmen	16	4–6	0–6
	Only from 1050 to 1149	Knights	Armoured	Superior	Undrilled	–	Lancers, Swordsmen	20	4–6	0–6
	Only from 1150	Knights	Heavily Armoured	Superior	Undrilled	–	Lancers, Swordsmen	23	4–6	0–12
German, Italian or other western knights and sergeants	Only before 1050	Cavalry	Armoured	Superior	Undrilled	–	Lancers, Swordsmen	16	4–6	0–8
	Only from 1050 to 1149	Knights	Armoured	Superior	Undrilled	–	Lancers, Swordsmen	20	4–6	
	Only from 1150	Knights	Heavily Armoured	Superior	Undrilled	–	Lancers, Swordsmen	23	4–6	
	Only from 1200	Knights	Heavily Armoured	Average	Drilled	–	Lancers, Swordsmen	21	4–6	
Hungarian, Pecheneg (Bessi), Cuman, Jazyges or other horse archers		Light Horse	Unprotected	Average	Undrilled	Bow	–	8	4–6	12–36
		Light Horse	Unprotected	Average	Undrilled	Bow	Swordsmen	10	4–6	
Szeklers		Light Horse	Unprotected	Superior	Undrilled	Bow	Swordsmen	12	4–6	0–18
				Average				10		
		Light Horse	Unprotected	Superior	Undrilled	Bow	Light Spear, Swordsmen	13		
				Average				11		
		Cavalry	Unprotected	Superior	Undrilled	Bow	Swordsmen	12		
			Unprotected	Average				10		
			Protected	Superior				14		
			Protected	Average				11		
		Cavalry	Unprotected	Superior	Undrilled	Bow*	Light Spear, Swordsmen	12		
			Unprotected	Average				10		
			Protected	Superior				14		
			Protected	Average				11		
Optional Troops									
Croat nobles	Only from 1097 to 1149	Cavalry	Armoured	Superior	Undrilled	–	Lancers, Swordsmen	16	4	0–4
		Cavalry	Armoured	Superior	Undrilled	–	Light Spear, Swordsmen	16	4	
	Only from 1150	Knights	Heavily Armoured	Superior	Undrilled	–	Lancers, Swordsmen	23	4	
Teutonic Order knights	Only from 1211 to 1225	Knights	Heavily Armoured	Superior	Drilled	–	Lancers, Swordsmen	26	2	0–2
Hungarian Slav, Croat or Serb spearmen		Heavy Foot	Protected	Average	Undrilled	–	Defensive Spearmen	6	6–8	0–12
				Poor				4		
Hungarian Slav, Croat or Serb foot archers		Medium Foot	Unprotected	Average	Undrilled	Bow	–	5	6–8	0–24
				Poor				3		
		Light Foot	Unprotected	Average	Undrilled	Bow	–	5	6–8	
				Poor				3		

Troop name		Troop Type				Capabilities		Points per base	Bases per BG	Total bases
		Type	Armour	Quality	Training	Shooting	Close Combat			
Croat axemen	Only from 1097	Medium Foot	Protected	Average	Undrilled	–	Light Spear, Swordsmen	6	4–6	0–6
Vlach foot		Medium Foot	Protected	Average	Undrilled	–	Light Spear	5	4–6	
Fortified camp								24		0–1
Allies										
Cuman allies (Only from 1239) – Cuman – See Field of Glory Companion 4: Swords and Scimitars: The Crusades										
Mongol allies (Only in 1285) – Tatar – See Field of Glory Companion 6: Eternal Empire: Byzantium at War										
Polish allies (Only from 1017 to 1116) – Early Polish – See Field of Glory Companion 8: Wolves from the Sea: The Dark Ages – or Feudal Polish										
Rus Allies (Only from 1019 to 1046) – Rus – See Field of Glory Companion 8: Wolves from the Sea: The Dark Ages										

EARLY HUNGARIAN ALLIES

Allied commander		Field Commander/Troop Commander						40/25		1
Troop name		Troop Type				Capabilities		Points per base	Bases per BG	Total bases
		Type	Armour	Quality	Training	Shooting	Close Combat			
Hungarian nobles and gentry	Only before 1200	Cavalry	Armoured	Superior	Undrilled	Bow*	Light Spear, Swordsmen	18	4	0–4
	Only before 1050	Cavalry	Armoured	Superior	Undrilled	–	Lancers, Swordsmen	16	4	
	Only from 1050 to 1149	Knights	Armoured	Superior	Undrilled	–	Lancers, Swordsmen	20	4	
	Only from 1150	Knights	Heavily Armoured	Superior	Undrilled	–	Lancers, Swordsmen	23	4	
German, Italian or other western knights and sergeants	Only before 1050	Cavalry	Armoured	Superior	Undrilled	–	Lancers, Swordsmen	16	4	0–4
	Only from 1050 to 1149	Knights	Armoured	Superior	Undrilled	–	Lancers, Swordsmen	20	4	
	Only from 1150	Knights	Heavily Armoured	Superior	Undrilled	–	Lancers, Swordsmen	23	4	
	Only from 1200	Knights	Heavily Armoured	Average	Drilled	–	Lancers, Swordsmen	21	4	
Hungarian, Pecheneg (Bessi), Cuman, Jazyges or other horse archers		Light Horse	Unprotected	Average	Undrilled	Bow	–	8	4–6	4–12
		Light Horse	Unprotected	Average	Undrilled	Bow	Swordsmen	10	4–6	
Szeklers		Light Horse	Unprotected	Superior	Undrilled	Bow	Swordsmen	12	4–6	0–6
				Average				10		
		Light Horse	Unprotected	Superior	Undrilled	Bow	Light Spear, Swordsmen	13	4–6	
				Average				11		
		Cavalry	Unprotected	Superior	Undrilled	Bow	Swordsmen	12		
			Unprotected	Average				10		
			Protected	Superior				14		
			Protected	Average				11		
		Cavalry	Unprotected	Superior	Undrilled	Bow*	Light Spear, Swordsmen	12		
			Unprotected	Average				10		
			Protected	Superior				14		
			Protected	Average				11		
Hungarian Slav, Croat or Serb spearmen		Heavy Foot	Protected	Average	Undrilled		Defensive Spearmen	6	4	0–4
				Poor				4		
Hungarian Slav, Croat or Serb foot archers		Medium Foot	Unprotected	Average	Undrilled	Bow	–	5	6–8	0–8
				Poor				3		
		Light Foot	Unprotected	Average	Undrilled	Bow	–	5	6–8	
				Poor				3		

Hungarian cavalry, by *Angus McBride*. Taken from Men-at-Arms 195: Hungary and the fall of Eastern Europe 1000–1568

TAIFA ANDALUSIAN

This list covers the armies of the Muslim Taifa kingdoms of the Iberian Peninsula from the break up of the Andalusian Caliphate until the Almoravid conquest. Armies of the Caliphate itself are covered by the Andalusian list in Field of Glory Companion 8: *Wolves from the Sea*.

In 1009 the Andalusian Caliphate was fragmented by internal conflicts, and finally abolished in 1031. The Andalusian state was divided into a number of small kingdoms called Taifa kingdoms. It was the start of the true *Reconquista*. The Taifa kingdoms fell into internal wars, and by the middle of the 11th century the larger kingdoms had conquered all the smaller ones. The Taifas of Sevilla, Zaragoza, Valencia and Murcia were the most important in this period. They fought among themselves and against the Christian kingdoms with the support of Christian mercenary troops and the Almoravids of North Africa.

This is the age of Rodrigo Diaz de Vivar – El Cid. He was a mercenary warlord and fought on the Muslim or Christian side at various times, often as commander.

Andalusian Archer

In 1086 the Christian advance alarmed the Andalusian Muslims, and they requested help from the Almoravids of North Africa. The Almoravids entered Al-Andalus in 1086 and defeated the Christians at Sagrajas the same year. They conquered all of the Andalusian kingdoms except Murcia, which resisted them until 1172 thanks to the recruitment of Christian mercenary troops.

TROOP NOTES

Almughavars were border soldiers, called Almogavari by the Muslims. They were used by Ibn Mardanish to defend the Taifa of Murcia, together with other mercenaries including Castilians, Aragonese and Franks.

"Slav" foot comprised the descendants of former mamluk (slave) foot of Christian origin. Following the collapse of the Andalusian Caliphate they ruled several Taifa kingdoms, including Valencia, Tortosa, Denia and Baleares. Most of these were small and lacked substantial armies. Following the capture of Valencia by the Taifa of Toledo in 1074, many fled to Murcia.

El Cid's mesnaderos were a veteran body that fought together for many years. They may therefore deserve Drilled status.

MURCIAN STARTER ARMY 1165 AD		
Commander-in-Chief	1	Field Commander
Sub-commanders	2	2 x Troop Commander
Christian mercenaries	2 BGs	Each comprising 4 bases of Christian mercenaries: Superior, Heavily Armoured, Undrilled Knights – Lancers, Swordsmen
Andalusian or Berber cavalry	3 BGs	Each comprising 4 bases of Andalusian or Berber light horse: Average, Unprotected, Undrilled Light Horse – Javelins, Light Spear
Andalusian spearmen	1 BG	8 bases of Andalusian spearmen: Average, Protected, Undrilled Heavy Foot – Defensive Spearmen
Christian spearmen	1 BG	8 bases of Christian spearmen: Average, Protected, Undrilled Heavy Foot – Defensive Spearmen
Almughavars	1 BG	8 bases of almughavars: Superior, Protected, Undrilled Medium Foot – Offensive Spearmen
Archers	1 BG	8 bases of archers: Average, Unprotected, Undrilled Light Foot – Bow
Camp	1	Unfortified camp
Total	9 BGs	Camp, 20 mounted bases, 32 foot bases, 3 commanders

BUILDING A CUSTOMISED LIST USING OUR ARMY POINTS

- Commanders should be depicted as Arab or Andalusian cavalry.
- Minima marked * only apply if any Christians are used.
- El Cid mesnaderos can only be used by the Taifa of Zaragoza if the C-in-C is "The Cid" (IC/FC).
- In the Taifa of Valencia from 1094 to 1101,

the C-in-C must be "The Cid" (IC/FC).
- All almughavars must be classified the same.
- Almoravid allies cannot be used with El Cid mesnaderos, Aragonese knights or other Christian troops.

Black Spearman

El Cid, by Angus McBride. Taken from Men-at-Arms 200: El Cid and the Reconquista 1050–1492

TAIFA ANDALUSIAN

Territory Types: Agricultural, Developed, Hilly

C-in-C		Inspired Commander/Field Commander/Troop Commander					80/50/35		1	
Sub-commanders		Field Commander					50		0–2	
		Troop Commander					35		0–3	

Troop name		Troop Type				Capabilities		Points per base	Bases per BG	Total bases
		Type	Armour	Quality	Training	Shooting	Close Combat			
Core Troops										
Andalusian or Berber cavalry		Light Horse	Unprotected	Average	Undrilled	Javelins	Light Spear	7	4–6	8–36
Andalusian spearmen		Heavy Foot	Protected	Average	Drilled	–	Defensive Spearmen	7	2/3 or all 8–12	8–24
					Undrilled			6		
Supporting archers		Light Foot	Unprotected	Average	Drilled or Undrilled	Bow	–	5	1/3 or 0	0–12
Separately deployed archers		Light Foot	Unprotected	Average	Drilled or Undrilled	Bow	–	5	6–8	8–24
				Poor				3		
		Medium Foot	Protected	Average	Drilled	Bow	–	7	6–8 0–24	
			Protected		Undrilled			6		
			Unprotected		Drilled			6		
			Unprotected		Undrilled			5		
Optional Troops										
Andalusian or other horse archers		Light Horse	Unprotected	Average	Drilled	Bow	–	8	4	0–4
Andalusian levy spearmen		Heavy Foot	Protected	Poor	Undrilled	–	Defensive Spearmen	5	2/3 or all 8–12	0–12
Supporting archers		Light Foot	Unprotected	Poor	Undrilled	Bow	–	3	1/3 or 0	0–6
Black spearmen		Medium Foot	Protected	Average	Undrilled	–	Light Spear	5	6–8	0–8
Berber spearmen		Heavy Foot	Protected	Average	Undrilled	–	Defensive Spearmen	6	2/3 or all 8–12	0–16
Supporting archers		Light Foot	Unprotected	Average	Undrilled	Bow	–	5	1/3 or 0	
Berber javelinmen		Light Foot	Unprotected	Average	Undrilled	Javelins	Light Spear	4	6–8	
Slingers		Light Foot	Unprotected	Average	Drilled or Undrilled	Sling	–	4	6–8	0–8
				Poor				2		
Fortified camp								24		0–1
Only Taifa of Seville (From 1023 to 1091) or Taifa Of Zaragoza (From 1017 to 1110)										
Arab cavalry		Cavalry	Armoured	Superior	Drilled	–	Lancers, Swordsmen	17	4–6	0–10
			Armoured	Average				13		
			Protected	Superior				13		
			Protected	Average				10		
Christian mercenaries	Only before 1050	Cavalry	Armoured	Superior	Undrilled	–	Lancers, Swordsmen	16	4	0–4
	Only from 1050	Knights	Armoured	Superior	Undrilled	–	Lancers, Swordsmen	20	4	
El Cid mesnaderos	Only Seville in 1079 or Zaragoza from 1081 to 1086	Knights	Armoured	Superior	Drilled	–	Lancers, Swordsmen	22	4	
					Undrilled			20		
Christian spearmen		Heavy Foot	Protected	Average	Undrilled	–	Defensive Spearmen	6	6–8	*8–16
Only Taifa of Murcia (From 1147 to 1172)										
Christian mercenaries	Only before 1150	Knights	Armoured	Superior	Undrilled	–	Lancers, Swordsmen	20	4–6	4–10
	Only from 1150	Knights	Heavily Armoured	Superior	Undrilled	–	Lancers, Swordsmen	23	4–6	
Christian spearmen		Heavy Foot	Protected	Average	Undrilled	–	Defensive Spearmen	6	6–8	8–20

TAIFA ANDALUSIAN

Troop name	Type	Armour	Quality	Training	Shooting	Close Combat	Points per base	Bases per BG	Total bases
Almughavars	Medium Foot	Protected	Superior	Undrilled	–	Impact Foot, Swordsmen	9	6–8	0–8
		Unprotected					7	6–8	
	Medium Foot	Protected	Superior	Undrilled	–	Offensive Spearmen	9	6–8	
		Unprotected					7	6–8	
"Slav" foot	Heavy Foot or Medium Foot	Armoured	Average	Drilled	–	Light Spear, Swordsmen	9	4–6	0–6
		Protected					7		
Only Taifa of Valencia (From 1094 to 1101)									
El Cid mesnaderos	Knights	Armoured	Superior	Drilled		Lancers, Swordsmen	22	4	4
				Undrilled			20		
Aragonese knights	Knights	Armoured	Superior	Undrilled		Lancers, Swordsmen	20	4	0–4
Christian spearmen	Heavy Foot	Protected	Average	Undrilled	–	Defensive Spearmen	6	6–8	8–16
Christian archers	Medium Foot	Protected	Average	Undrilled	Bow	–	6	4–6	0–6
Allies									
Almoravid Allies (Only from 1039) – Fanatic Berber									

TAIFA ANDALUSIAN ALLIES

Allied commander	Field Commander/Troop Commander						40/25	1	
Troop name	**Troop Type**				**Capabilities**		**Points per base**	**Bases per BG**	**Total bases**
	Type	Armour	Quality	Training	Shooting	Close Combat			
Andalusian or Berber cavalry	Light Horse	Unprotected	Average	Undrilled	Javelins	Light Spear	7	4–6	4–12
Andalusian spearmen	Heavy Foot	Protected	Average	Drilled	–	Defensive Spearmen	7	2/3 or all	4–8
				Undrilled			6	8–12	
Supporting archers	Light Foot	Unprotected	Average	Drilled or Undrilled	Bow	–	5	1/3 or 0	0–4
Separately deployed archers	Light Foot	Unprotected	Average	Drilled or Undrilled	Bow	–	5	6–8	3–8
			Poor				3		
	Medium Foot	Protected	Average	Drilled	Bow	–	7	6–8	0–8
		Unprotected					6		
Andalusian levy spearmen	Heavy Foot	Protected	Poor	Undrilled	–	Defensive Spearmen	5	2/3 or all	0–4
Supporting archers	Light Foot	Unprotected	Poor	Undrilled	Bow	–	3	1/3 or 0	4–6	0–2
Berber spearmen	Heavy Foot	Protected	Average	Undrilled	–	Defensive Spearmen	6	2/3 or all	0–6
Supporting archers	Light Foot	Unprotected	Average	Undrilled	Bow	–	5	1/3 or 0	6
Berber javelinmen	Light Foot	Unprotected	Average	Undrilled	Javelins	Light Spear	4	4–6	
Only Taifa of Seville (From 1023 to 1091) or Taifa Of Zaragoza (From 1017 to 1110)									
Arab cavalry	Cavalry	Armoured	Superior	Drilled	–	Lancers, Swordsmen	17	4	0–4
		Armoured	Average				13		
		Protected	Superior				13		
		Protected	Average				10		
Christian spearmen	Heavy Foot	Protected	Average	Undrilled	–	Defensive Spearmen	6	4–6	0–6
Only Taifa of Murcia (From 1147 to 1172)									
Christian mercenaries	Only before 1150	Knights	Armoured	Superior	Undrilled		Lancers, Swordsmen	20	4	0–4
	Only from 1150	Knights	Heavily Armoured	Superior	Undrilled		Lancers, Swordsmen	23	4	
Christian spearmen	Heavy Foot	Protected	Average	Undrilled	–	Defensive Spearmen	6	4–6	0–6
Only Taifa of Valencia (From 1094 to 1101)									
Christian spearmen	Heavy Foot	Protected	Average	Undrilled	–	Defensive Spearmen	6	4–6	0–6

Andalusian cavalry, by Angus McBride. Taken from Men-at-Arms 348: The Moors

FEUDAL NAVARRESE AND ARAGONESE

After the death of Sancho III in 1035 AD, his possessions were split between his four sons. Ramiro I received the county of Aragon, now converted into a brand new kingdom. Garcia Sánchez II became the new king of Navarre. Fernando inherited the County of Castille, and soon became King of León after a short civil war against Bermudo III. Gonzalo Sánchez received the counties of Sobrarbe and Ribagorza, also converted into a kingdom, but it was incorporated into Aragon at his death ten years later.

Navarre and Aragon were re-united under Sancho Ramirez in 1076. In the following years the kingdom successfully expanded to the south following the Ebro valley, especially under Alfonso I the Battler who defeated the Almoravids at Cutanda (1120) and Cullera (1126) and conquered Saragossa in 1118 with the support of French crusaders. At his death following the siege of Fraga (1134), the two kingdoms definitively split. Ramiro of Aragon betrothed his daughter Petronila to Ramon Berenguer IV of Barcelona in 1137. The dynastic union with Catalonia is the starting point of the Crown of Aragon which is covered in a separate list.

Sancho VI of Navarre, seeing the kingdom menaced by Castile and the Crown of Aragon, made new alliances with his northern neighbours; he married his daughter Berenguela to Richard I of England and his daughter Blanca to Theobald of Champagne. His son Sancho VII the Strong played a major role in the decisive victory over the Muwahhidun (Almohades) at Las Navas de Tolosa (1212) beside the kings of Castile and Catalonia-Aragon. He was succeeded by Theobald IV of Champagne and I of Navarre, who started a new dynasty with strong French connections, including a temporary union with France resulting from the marriage of Juana I to Philip IV of France in 1286, and lasting until the death of Charles IV of France and I of Navarre in 1328. Having no male heir, his daughter Juana became the new queen of Navarre, while the French crown passed to his cousin Philip de Valois against the candidature of his nephew Edward III of England. This succession was the origin of the 100 Years War that was to start nine years later.

This list covers Aragonese armies from 1035 until the dynastic union with Catalonia in 1147, and Navarrese armies from 1035 to 1328.

TROOP NOTES

Navarre was the first Christian state in the Iberian Peninsula to lose contact with Muslim territories as its expansion to the south was blocked by Castile and Aragon. Therefore its army was less influenced by Muslim warfare. On the other hand, there were strong connections with the south-west of modern France from quite early on, and French crusaders participated in different campaigns against the Moors. After the union with France, Navarre was not involved in any major conflict.

The military orders in the Iberian Peninsula were more numerous than those of other countries, but their knights were on some occasions less controllable, hence the option to grade them as Undrilled. They cannot be used after the union with France in 1286.

A proportion of the army's spearmen, crossbowmen or archers can be Mudejars (Muslims) or Jews conscripted from the formerly Muslim areas. This does not affect their classification.

Javelinman

NAVARRESE STARTER ARMY 1175 AD		
Commander-in-Chief	1	Field Commander
Sub-commanders	2	2 x Troop Commander
Knights	3 BGs	Each comprising 4 bases of knights: Superior, Heavily Armoured, Undrilled Knights – Lancers, Swordsmen
Basque cavalry	2 BGs	Each comprising 4 bases of Basque cavalry: Average, Unprotected, Undrilled Light Horse – Javelins, Light Spear
Spearmen	2 BGs	Each comprising 6 bases of spearmen: Average, Protected, Undrilled Heavy Foot – Defensive Spearmen
Javelinmen	3 BGs	Each comprising 6 bases of javelinmen: Average, Unprotected, Undrilled Light Foot – Javelins, Light Spear
Camp	1	Unfortified camp
Total	10 BGs	Camp, 20 mounted bases, 30 foot bases, 3 commanders

BUILDING A CUSTOMISED LIST USING OUR ARMY POINTS

Choose an army based on the maxima and minima in the list below. The following special instructions apply to this army:

- Commanders should be depicted as knights.

Slinger

FEUDAL NAVARRESE AND ARAGONESE									
Territory Types: Agricultural, Hilly, Mountains									
C-in-C		Inspired Commander/Field Commander/Troop Commander					80/50/35	1	
Sub-commanders		Field Commander					50	0–2	
		Troop Commander					35	0–3	
Troop name		**Troop Type**				**Capabilities**	Points per base	Bases per BG	Total bases
		Type	Armour	Quality	Training	Shooting	Close Combat		
Core Troops									
Knights	Only before 1050	Cavalry	Armoured	Superior	Undrilled	–	Lancers, Swordsmen	16	4–6	6–36
	Only from 1050 to 1149	Knights	Armoured	Superior	Undrilled	–	Lancers, Swordsmen	20	4–6	6–32
	Only from 1150	Knights	Heavily Armoured	Superior	Undrilled	–	Lancers, Swordsmen	23	4–6	6–26
Javelinmen		Medium Foot	Protected	Average	Undrilled	–	Light Spear	5	6–8	12–40
			Unprotected					4		
		Light Foot	Unprotected	Average	Undrilled	Javelins	Light Spear	4	6–8	
Spearmen		Heavy Foot	Protected	Average	Undrilled	–	Defensive Spearmen	6	6–8	6–18
Optional Troops									
Basque cavalry or mercenary Berber light horse		Light Horse	Unprotected	Average	Undrilled	Javelins	Light Spear	7	4–6	0–12
Military Orders knights	Only from 1110 to 1149	Knights	Armoured	Superior	Drilled	–	Lancers, Swordsmen	22	4–6	0–6
					Undrilled			20		
	Only from 1150 to 1286	Knights	Heavily Armoured	Superior	Drilled	–	Lancers, Swordsmen	26	4–6	
					Undrilled			23		
Military order spearmen	Only from 1110 to 1286	Heavy Foot	Protected	Average	Drilled	–	Defensive Spearmen	7	4–6	0–6
			Armoured					9		
Military order crossbowmen		Medium Foot	Protected	Average	Drilled	Crossbow	–	7	4–6	0–6
Crossbowmen		Medium Foot	Protected	Average	Undrilled	Crossbow	–	6	6–8	Before 1150 0–8, From 1150 0–16
				Poor				4		
		Light Foot	Unprotected	Average	Undrilled	Crossbow	–	5	6–8	
Archers		Medium Foot	Protected	Average	Undrilled	Bow	–	6	6–8	0–8
			Protected	Poor				4		
			Unprotected	Average				5		
			Unprotected	Poor				3		
		Light Foot	Unprotected	Average	Undrilled	Bow	–	5	6–8	
Slingers		Light Foot	Unprotected	Average	Undrilled	Sling	–	4	4–6	0–8
Fortified camp								24		0–1
Allies									
Aragonese allies (Only Navarrese from 1045 to 1070) – Feudal Navarrese and Aragonese									
French crusader allies – Feudal French									

FEUDAL NAVARRESE AND ARAGONESE ALLIES									
Allied commander			Field Commander/Troop Commander				40/25		1
Troop name		Troop Type				Capabilities		Points per base	Bases per BG	Total bases
		Type	Armour	Quality	Training	Shooting	Close Combat			
Knights	Only before 1050	Cavalry	Armoured	Superior	Undrilled	–	Lancers, Swordsmen	16	4–6	4–8
	Only from 1050 to 1149	Knights	Armoured	Superior	Undrilled	–	Lancers, Swordsmen	20	4–6	
	Only from 1150	Knights	Heavily Armoured	Superior	Undrilled	–	Lancers, Swordsmen	23	4–6	
Javelinmen		Medium Foot	Protected	Average	Undrilled	–	Light Spear	5	4–8	4–12
			Unprotected					4		
		Light Foot	Unprotected	Average	Undrilled	Javelins	Light Spear	4	4–8	
Spearmen		Heavy Foot	Protected	Average	Undrilled	–	Defensive Spearmen	6	4–6	0–6
Basque cavalry or mercenary Berber light horse		Light Horse	Unprotected	Average	Undrilled	Javelins	Light Spear	7	4	0–4
Crossbowmen	Only from 1150	Medium Foot	Protected	Average	Undrilled	Crossbow	–	6	4–6	0–6
				Poor	Undrilled			4		
		Light Foot	Unprotected	Average	Undrilled	Crossbow	–	5	4–6	

FEUDAL CASTILIAN, LEONESE OR PORTUGUESE

Fernando I, Count of Castile, was crowned king of León after killing the Leonese king Bermudo III in the battle of Tamarón in 1037 AD. At his death, Fernando split his possessions between his sons: Sancho II received Castile, now converted into a brand new kingdom, Alfonso VI received León, and Garcia received Galicia. From then on Castile and León were re-united and split again on several occasions until the definitive union into the Crown of Castile-León made by Fernando III the Saint in 1230.

This list covers the armies of Castile and León from the victory of Fernando I of Castile over Bermudo II of León until the definitive re-union of both states, and the subsequent Crown of Castile-León until the accession of Pedro I the Cruel in 1350. It also covers Portuguese armies from the foundation of the kingdom in 1139 until the accession of Pedro I of Portugal in 1357.

During this period Castile played a central role in the politics of the Iberian Peninsula. At one time or another it allied with or fought against most of its neighbours, both Christian and Muslim, and suffered several civil wars. Nevertheless it consolidated its position as the dominant power in the peninsula after the final union with León in 1230, while Portugal controlled the westernmost part of it and the Crown of Aragon diverted its political expansion to the Mediterranean after conquering Valencia.

Many important battles were fought during these turbulent times. The conquest of Toledo in 1085 provoked the arrival of the Almoravids in the Iberian Peninsula, responding to the request for help sent by the Muslim Taifa kingdoms. The Almoravids achieved important victories against Castile-León at Zalaca (1086), Consuegra (1097), Salatrices (1106) and Uclés (1108), but never managed to recover Toledo. To the west, they were defeated at Ourique (1139) by Alfonso I of Portugal, who conquered Lisbon in 1147.

The Almoravids were replaced by the Muwahhidun (Almohades) from 1146, who defeated the Castilians again at Alarcos (1195). In 1212 a Crusade was called to definitively crush Muslim power in the peninsula. The European Crusaders abandoned the expedition after the conquest of Calatrava due to the scanty booty taken, but the combined armies of Alfonso VIII of Castile, Pere II of Aragon (I of Catalonia) and Sancho VII of Navarre inflicted such a severe defeat on the Muwahhidun that they would never recover. A couple of years later Fernando III of Castile-León conquered Cordova, Jaén and Seville, Portugal conquered the Algarve, and Muslim territories in modern Spain were rapidly reduced to the Kingdom of Granada in the extreme south.

Spearman

TROOP NOTES

The military orders in the Iberian Peninsula were more numerous than those of other countries, but their knights were on some occasions less controllable, hence the option to grade them as Undrilled.

While there were probably at least some light horse from quite early on, they were not called jinetes until their numbers greatly expanded during the 13th century. They can include both Muslims, mostly Berbers, and Christians.

Caballeros villanos were non-noble knights supplied by the cities as a core part of their militia forces. In areas reconquered from the Moors they may have retained their customary fighting style.

A proportion of the army's spearmen, crossbowmen or archers can be Mudejars (Muslims) or Jews conscripted from the formerly Muslim areas. This does not affect their classification.

FEUDAL CASTILIAN STARTER ARMY 1225 AD		
Commander-in-Chief	1	Troop Commander
Sub-commanders	2	2 x Troop Commander
Military Order knights	1 BG	4 bases of Military Order knights: Superior, Heavily Armoured, Drilled Knights – Lancers, Swordsmen
Feudal knights	2 BGs	Each comprising 4 bases of feudal knights: Superior, Heavily Armoured, Undrilled Knights – Lancers, Swordsmen
Caballeros villanos	1 BG	4 bases of caballeros villanos: Average, Armoured, Undrilled Cavalry – Lancers, Swordsmen
Jinetes	1 BG	4 bases of jinetes: Average, Unprotected, Undrilled Light Horse – Javelins, Light Spear
Spearmen	2 BGs	Each comprising 6 bases of spearmen: Average, Protected, Undrilled Heavy Foot – Defensive Spearmen
Crossbowmen	1 BG	6 bases of crossbowmen: Average, Unprotected, Undrilled Light Foot – Crossbow
Slingers	1 BG	6 bases of slingers: Average, Unprotected, Undrilled Light Foot – Sling
Camp	1	Unfortified camp
Total	9 BGs	Camp, 20 mounted bases, 24 foot bases, 3 commanders

BUILDING A CUSTOMISED LIST USING OUR ARMY POINTS

Choose an army based on the maxima and minima in the list below. The following special instructions apply to this army:

• Commanders should be depicted as knights.

Archer

FEUDAL CASTILIAN, LEONESE OR PORTUGUESE

Territory Types: Agricultural, Developed, Hilly

C-in-C	Inspired Commander/Field Commander/Troop Commander						80/50/35	1
Sub-commanders	Field Commander						50	0–2
	Troop Commander						35	0–3

Troop name		Troop Type				Capabilities		Points per base	Bases per BG	Total bases
		Type	Armour	Quality	Training	Shooting	Close Combat			
Core Troops										
Feudal knights	Only before 1050	Cavalry	Armoured	Superior	Undrilled	–	Lancers, Swordsmen	16	4–6	6–36
	Only from 1050 to 1149	Knights	Armoured	Superior	Undrilled	–	Lancers, Swordsmen	20	4–6	6–30
	Only from 1150	Knights	Heavily Armoured	Superior	Undrilled	–	Lancers, Swordsmen	23	4–6	6–26
Caballeros villanos	Any date	Cavalry	Armoured	Average	Undrilled	–	Lancers, Swordsmen	12	4–6	0–8
	Only from 1050	Knights	Armoured	Average	Undrilled	–	Lancers, Swordsmen	16	4–6	
Military order knights	Only from 1100 to 1149	Knights	Armoured	Superior	Drilled	–	Lancers, Swordsmen	22	4–6	0–8
					Undrilled			20		
	Only from 1150	Knights	Heavily Armoured	Superior	Drilled	–	Lancers, Swordsmen	26	4–6	
					Undrilled			23		
Spearmen		Heavy Foot	Protected	Average	Undrilled	–	Defensive Spearmen	6	6–8	6–24
				Poor				4		
Jinetes	Only from 1200	Light Horse	Unprotected	Average	Undrilled	Javelins	Light Spear	7	4–6	4–12
	Only from 1300	Light Horse	Protected	Average	Undrilled	Javelins	Light Spear	8	4–6	
Optional Troops										
Basque or mercenary Berber light horse		Light Horse	Unprotected	Average	Drilled	Javelins	Light Spear	7	4–6	0–6
Mounted crossbowmen	Only from 1150	Light Horse	Unprotected	Average	Drilled	Crossbow	–	7	4–6	0–6
			Protected					8		
Javelinmen		Medium Foot	Protected	Average	Undrilled	–	Light Spear	5	6–8	0–18
			Unprotected					4	6–8	
		Light Foot	Unprotected	Average	Undrilled	Javelins	Light Spear	4	6–8	
Crossbowmen		Medium Foot	Protected	Average	Undrilled	Crossbow	–	6	6–8	Before 1150 0–8, From 1150 0–16
				Poor				4		
		Light Foot	Unprotected	Average	Undrilled	Crossbow	–	5	6–8	
Archers		Medium Foot	Protected	Average	Undrilled	Bow	–	6	6–8	0–12
			Protected	Poor				4		
			Unprotected	Average				5		
			Unprotected	Poor				3		
		Light Foot	Unprotected	Average	Undrilled	Bow	–	5	6–8	

Slingers		Light Foot	Unprotected	Average	Undrilled	Sling	–	4	6–8	0–12
Military order spearmen	Only from 1100	Heavy Foot	Protected	Average	Drilled	–	Defensive Spearmen	7	6–8	0–8
			Armoured					9		
Military order crossbowmen		Medium Foot	Protected	Average	Drilled	Crossbow	–	7	4–6	0–6
Fortified camp								24		0–1
Allies										
Navarrese allies (Only if Castilian) – Feudal Navarrese and Aragonese										
Catalano–Aragonese allies (Only if Castilian after 1135) – Feudal Catalan and Early Crown of Aragon										
Portuguese allies (Only if Castilian after 1140) – Feudal Castilian, Leonese or Portuguese										
Granadine allies (Only if Castilian after 1238) – Early Granadine										
Marinid allies (Only after 1269) – Fanatic Berber										

FEUDAL CASTILIAN, LEONESE OR PORTUGUESE ALLIES

Allied commander		Field Commander/Troop Commander						40/25		1
Troop name		**Troop Type**				**Capabilities**		**Points per base**	**Bases per BG**	**Total bases**
		Type	Armour	Quality	Training	Shooting	Close Combat			
Feudal knights	Only before 1050	Cavalry	Armoured	Superior	Undrilled	–	Lancers, Swordsmen	16	4–6	4–8
	Only from 1050 to 1149	Knights	Armoured	Superior	Undrilled	–	Lancers, Swordsmen	20	4–6	
	Only from 1150	Knights	Heavily Armoured	Superior	Undrilled	–	Lancers, Swordsmen	23	4–6	
Caballeros villanos	Any date	Cavalry	Armoured	Average	Undrilled	–	Lancers, Swordsmen	12	4	4–12
	Only from 1050	Knights	Armoured	Average	Undrilled	–	Lancers, Swordsmen	16	4	0–4
Military order knights	Only from 1100 to 1149	Knights	Armoured	Superior	Drilled	–	Lancers, Swordsmen	22	4	0–4
					Undrilled			20		
	Only from 1150	Knights	Heavily Armoured	Superior	Drilled	–	Lancers, Swordsmen	26	4	
					Undrilled			23		
Spearmen		Heavy Foot	Protected	Average	Undrilled	–	Defensive Spearmen	6	6–8	0–8
				Poor				4		
Jinetes	Only from 1200	Light Horse	Unprotected	Average	Undrilled	Javelins	Light Spear	7	4	0–4
	Only from 1300	Light Horse	Protected	Average	Undrilled	Javelins	Light Spear	8	4	
Javelinmen		Medium Foot	Protected	Average	Undrilled	–	Light Spear	5	4–6	0–6
			Unprotected					4	4–6	
		Light Foot	Unprotected	Average	Undrilled	Javelins	Light Spear	4	4–6	
Crossbowmen	Only from 1150	Medium Foot	Protected	Average	Undrilled	Crossbow	–	6	4–6	0–8
				Poor	Undrilled			4		
		Light Foot	Unprotected	Average	Undrilled	Crossbow	–	5	4–6	
Archers		Medium Foot	Protected	Average	Undrilled	Bow	–	6	4	0–8
			Protected	Poor				4		
			Unprotected	Average				5		
			Unprotected	Poor				3		
		Light Foot	Unprotected	Average	Undrilled	Bow	–	5	4	
Slingers		Light Foot	Unprotected	Average	Undrilled	Sling	–	4	4	

FANATIC BERBER

Arising circa 1039 AD, the Murabit (Almoravid) sect was considered the most fanatical faction in the Islamic world. Its ideology spread among the tribes of Sub-Saharan Africa within a few years, then to North West Africa, forming the Almoravid Empire. In 1086, the Almoravids entered Spain in response to a plea for aid from al-Mutamid, king of the Taifa of Seville, following the conquest of Toledo by Alfonso VI in 1085. The Christians were defeated at the Battle of Sagrajas (1086) and the Almoravids quickly took control of the south of the peninsula, defeating and annexing one by one all the Taifa kingdoms.

From 1130 to 1149 the Almohades conquered North Africa from the Almoravids. They invaded the Iberian peninsula in 1145, transferring their capital to Seville in 1170 and capturing the surviving Taifa of Murcia in 1172. After their victory over Christian troops at Alarcos in 1195, the Christians organized a counter-attack in 1212, designated a Crusade by the Pope. The Almohades were defeated at the Battle of Navas de Tolosa and driven south. Only the Emirate of Granada under the Nasrid dynasty and an epidemic of disease stopped the Christians from conquering the whole peninsula.

By 1269 the Almohades were replaced in Africa by the Marinid dynasty. The Marinids supported the Emirate of Granada in its war against the Christians in Spain until their defeat by the Hafsids in 1465.

Following the fall of the Almohad Empire the Marinids coexisted with two other dynasties in North West Africa: The Abdalwadids ruled Algeria until 1550 with two short periods of Marinid occupation (1337–1348 and 1352–1359). The Hafsids ruled Tunisia until 1574, also with a short period of Marinid occupation. The Crown of Aragon established a protectorate over Hafsid Tunisia and the Hafsids used Catalan mercenaries against the main Marinid power as well as their Abdalwadid neighbours.

This list covers Almoravid (Murabit) armies from 1039 to 1146, Almohad armies from 1130 to 1269, Marinid armies from 1248 to 1465, Abdalwadid armies from 1236 to 1500 and Hafsid armies from 1229 to 1500.

TROOP NOTES

Black Guard were usually deployed in the rear. Lamtuna and Hintata were tribal troops, but were trained to fight in close formation with long spears, and were considered the best infantry in the Almoravid and Almohad armies. Lamtuna covered their faces with veils. Andalusian infantry were used as sacrificial troops to blunt the charges of the Christian knights. At Sagrajas 4,000 Black Africans with javelins and sword were used by the Almoravids to attack the Christian camp. We assume that these were similar to Black troops used by the Fatimids.

Sagrajas was the first battle in Spain in which camels were used – with great success against the Christian knights. "Ghuzz" mercenaries were probably Turcomans. Arab cavalry were the Almohades' response to Christian knights. They were not used in Africa. Christian mercenaries were used in Africa but not in Spain.

Black Guard

ALMOHAD STARTER ARMY 1175 AD		
Commander-in-Chief	1	Field Commander
Sub-commanders	2	2 x Troop Commander
Berber or Andalusian cavalry	3 BGs	Each comprising 4 bases of Andalusian or Berber cavalry: Average, Unprotected, Undrilled Light Horse – Javelins, Light Spear
Arab cavalry	1 BG	4 bases of Arab cavalry: Average, Armoured, Undrilled Cavalry – Lancers, Swordsmen
Camelry	1 BG	4 bases of camelry: Average, Protected, Undrilled Camelry – Lancers, Swordsmen
Lamtuna or Hintata spearmen	1 BG	8 bases of Lamtuna or Hintata spearmen: Superior, Protected, Drilled Heavy Foot – Offensive Spearmen
Other Berber or Black spearmen	3 BGs	Each comprising 8 bases of other Berber or Black spearmen: Average, Protected, Undrilled Heavy Foot – Defensive Spearmen
Berber or Black javelinmen	1 BG	8 bases of javelinmen: Average, Unprotected, Undrilled Light Foot – Javelins, Light Spear
Berber or Black archers	1 BG	8 bases of archers: Average, Unprotected, Undrilled Light Foot – Bow
Camp	1	Unfortified camp
Total	11 BGs	Camp, 20 mounted bases, 48 foot bases, 3 commanders

BUILDING A CUSTOMISED LIST USING OUR ARMY POINTS

Choose an army based on the maxima and minima in the list below. The following special instructions apply to this army:

- Commanders should be depicted as Berber cavalry.
- As usual, supporting archers must be of the same Quality as the spearmen in their battle group.

- Christian mercenaries and almughavars cannot be used with Andalusians or Camelry.
- Abdalwadid and Hafsid armies cannot include Andalusians.

Camel Rider

FANATIC BERBER

Territory Types: Agricultural, Hilly, Desert

Troop name		Troop Type				Capabilities		Points per base	Bases per BG	Total bases
C-in-C		Inspired Commander/Field Commander/Troop Commander						80/50/35	1	
Sub-commanders		Field Commander						50	0–2	
		Troop Commander						35	0–3	
		Type	Armour	Quality	Training	Shooting	Close Combat			
Core Troops										
Berber or Andalusian cavalry		Light Horse	Unprotected	Average	Undrilled	Javelins	Light Spear	7	4–6	12–42
Lamtuna or Hintata spearmen	Only Almoravids or Almohades	Heavy Foot	Protected	Superior	Drilled	–	Offensive Spearmen	10	2/3 or all	0–18
				Average				8		
Supporting archers		Light Foot	Unprotected	Superior	Drilled	Bow	–	6	1/3 or 0	0–9
				Average				5		
Other Berber or Black spearmen		Heavy Foot	Protected	Average	Undrilled	–	Defensive Spearmen	6	2/3 or all	16–48
Supporting archers		Light Foot	Unprotected	Average	Undrilled	Bow	–	5	1/3 or 0	0–24
Separately deployed Berber or Black archers		Light Foot	Unprotected	Average	Undrilled	Bow	–	5	6–8	0–24
		Medium Foot	Unprotected	Average	Undrilled	Bow	–	5	6–8	
Berber or Black javelinmen		Light Foot	Unprotected	Average	Undrilled	Javelins	Light Spear	4	6–8	6–40
Optional Troops										
"Black Guard"	Only Almoravids, Almohades or Hafsids	Heavy Foot	Protected	Superior	Drilled	–	Defensive Spearmen	9	6–8	0–8
Arab cavalry	Only Almohades	Cavalry	Armoured	Average	Undrilled	–	Lancers, Swordsmen	12	4–6	0–12
			Protected					9		
"Ghuzz" mercenaries		Light Horse	Unprotected	Average	Undrilled	Bow	Swordsmen	10	4	0–4
		Cavalry	Unprotected	Average	Undrilled	Bow	Swordsmen	10		
			Protected					11		
Christian mercenary knights and sergeants	Only Almoravids	Knights	Armoured	Superior	Undrilled	–	Lancers, Swordsmen	20	4–6	0–6
	Only Hafsids	Knights	Heavily Armoured	Superior	Undrilled	–	Lancers, Swordsmen	23	4–6	
Camelry		Camelry	Protected	Average	Undrilled	–	Lancers, Swordsmen	11	4–6	0–6
Andalusian spearmen		Heavy Foot	Protected	Poor	Undrilled	–	Defensive Spearmen	4	2/3 or all	0–24
Supporting archers		Light Foot	Unprotected	Poor	Undrilled	Bow	–	3	1/3 or 0	0–12
Black swordsmen	Only Almoravids	Heavy Foot	Protected	Average	Drilled	–	Light Spear, Swordsmen	7	2/3 or all	0–16
Supporting archers		Light Foot	Unprotected	Average	Drilled	Bow	–	5	1/3 or 0	0–8
Slingers		Light Foot	Unprotected	Average	Undrilled	Sling	–	4	6–8	0–8
				Poor				2		
Arab crossbowmen		Light Foot	Unprotected	Average	Undrilled	Crossbow	–	5	6–8	0–8
Christian mercenary crossbowmen	Only Almoravids or Hafsids	Medium Foot	Protected	Average	Drilled	Crossbow	–	7	4	0–4
					Undrilled			6		
Mercenary almughavars	Only Hafsids from 1269 to 1350	Medium Foot	Unprotected	Superior	Undrilled	–	Offensive Spearmen	7	4–6	0–6
			Protected					9		
		Medium Foot	Unprotected	Superior	Undrilled	–	Impact Foot, Swordsmen	7		
			Protected					9		
Fortified camp								24		0–1
Allies										
Andalusian allies (Only Almoravids in Spain) – Taifa Andalusian										

FANATIC BERBER ALLIES

Allied commander		Field Commander/Troop Commander						40/25	1	
Troop name		**Troop Type**				**Capabilities**		**Points per base**	**Bases per BG**	**Total bases**
		Type	Armour	Quality	Training	Shooting	Close Combat			
Berber or Andalusian cavalry		Light Horse	Unprotected	Average	Undrilled	Javelins	Light Spear	7	4–6	4–12
Lamtuna or Hintata spearmen	Only Almoravids or Almohades	Heavy Foot	Protected	Superior	Drilled	–	Offensive Spearmen	10	2/3 or all	0–6
				Average				8		
Supporting archers		Light Foot	Unprotected	Superior	Drilled	Bow	–	6	1/3 or 0 (6–9)	0–3
				Average				5		
Other Berber or Black spearmen		Heavy Foot	Protected	Average	Undrilled	–	Defensive Spearmen	6	2/3 or all	4–12
Supporting archers		Light Foot	Unprotected	Average	Undrilled	Bow	–	5	1/3 or 0 (6–12)	0–6
Separately deployed Berber or Black archers		Light Foot	Unprotected	Average	Undrilled	Bow	–	5	6–8	0–8
		Medium Foot	Unprotected	Average	Undrilled	Bow	–	5	6–8	
Berber or Black javelinmen		Light Foot	Unprotected	Average	Undrilled	Javelins	Light Spear	4	6–8	0–12
Arab cavalry	Only Almohades	Cavalry	Armoured	Average	Undrilled	–	Lancers, Swordsmen	12	4	0–4
			Protected					9		
Andalusian spearmen		Heavy Foot	Protected	Poor	Undrilled	–	Defensive Spearmen	4	2/3 or all	0–8
Supporting archers		Light Foot	Unprotected	Poor	Undrilled	Bow	–	3	1/3 or 0 (6–12)	0–4
Black swordsmen	Only Almoravids	Heavy Foot	Protected	Average	Drilled	–	Light Spear, Swordsmen	7	2/3 or all	0–6
Supporting archers		Light Foot	Unprotected	Average	Drilled	Bow	–	5	1/3 or 0 (6–9)	0–3

ITALO-NORMAN

The Normans first appeared in southern Italy in 1017 as mercenaries fighting for the Lombard princes in rebellion against the Byzantine Catapanate of Italy and subsequently also fought for the Byzantines. In 1030 the Norman leader Ranulf Drengot was granted the County of Aversa, north of Naples, by Sergius IV of Naples, his title being recognised by the Holy Roman Emperor Konrad II in 1038.

Encouraged by Ranulf's success, more Normans arrived in Italy. From 1038 to 1040 they fought along with the Lombards as mercenaries for the Byzantines against the Arabs in Sicily. Soon after, the Lombards once again revolted against the Byzantines, joined by the Normans. In 1041 the Norman-Lombard army defeated the Byzantines at Olivento, Montemaggiore and Montepeloso. In 1042 the Normans were assigned fiefs around Melfi by Gaimar of Salerno, with William de Hauteville as their Count. From then on, though maintaining their firm alliance with Gaimar until his death, the Normans warred against the Byzantines to expand their own territories rather than on behalf of the Lombards. In 1047, William's brother and successor Drogo was recognised as "Duke and Master of Italy and Count

Feudal Knight

of the Normans of all Apulia and Calabria" by the Holy Roman Emperor Heinrich III.

By 1053 the Pope had had enough of Norman depredations and made war on them in alliance with the Byzantines. At the Battle of Civitate, however, the Normans under Humphrey de Hauteville (Count of Apulia following his brother Drogo's assassination), and Richard Drengot (Count of Aversa), defeated the Papal forces before they could join up with their Byzantine allies.

In 1057 Humphrey died, and was succeeded by another brother, Robert Guiscard (The Cunning). Switching allegiance from the Holy Roman Emperor to the Pope, in 1059 Robert Guiscard was recognised by the Pope as Duke of Apulia, Calabria and Sicily, and Richard of Aversa

as Prince of Capua, which he had captured the previous year.

Guiscard, with yet another brother, Roger, subsequently conquered the whole of Apulia and Calabria, expelling the last Byzantine forces by 1071, and conquering the last of the Lombard principalities by 1077. Arab Sicily was invaded and Messina, near the north-eastern corner, was captured in 1061. The main Arab army was defeated at the Battle of Misilmeri in 1068. Palermo was captured in 1072, and Roger was invested by his brother as Count of Sicily.

In 1081 Guiscard, together with his eldest son Bohemond, shipped his army across the Adriatic to invade the Byzantine Empire and defeated the Emperor Alexios Komnenos outside Dyrrhachium. The city held out until the following year, but after

Italo-Norman troops landing, by Angus McBride. Taken from Elite 9: The Normans

its fall, Guiscard swiftly gained control of Illyria and advanced into Macedonia. Before he could advance further, however, he was forced to return to Italy to rescue Pope Gregory, who was under attack by the Holy Roman Emperor Heinrich IV. He was absent from Greece for two years, during the first of which Bohemond continued the Norman advance until all of Macedonia and part of Thessaly were under his control. In 1083, however, Alexios managed to turn the tide, and by the end of that year almost all of the Norman gains had been lost. In 1084 the Emperor Heinrich retreated hastily from Rome on the approach of Guiscard's army, and the Pope was rescued. On his way back to join Bohemond in Greece in 1085, Guiscard contracted a fever and died.

He was succeeded as Duke by Roger Borsa, his son by his second wife, with the support of Roger of Sicily – the claim of Bohemond being passed over. Bohemond rebelled, but eventually terms were reached, Bohemond being made Prince of Taranto. He subsequently took a major part in the First Crusade, making himself Prince of Antioch after the capture of that city by the Crusaders.

The conquest of Sicily was completed by Count Roger between 1085 and 1091. In 1127 Roger II of Sicily succeeded to the Duchy of Apulia and Calabria, uniting all the Norman possessions in Italy under one rule. In 1130 he was created King of Sicily by the Anti-Pope Anacletus II. He died in 1154 and was succeeded by his son William the Bad.

This list covers the armies of the Normans in Italy and Sicily from 1041 until 1154.

TROOP NOTES

Sicilian Greek troops (known as "Griffons" to Richard the Lionheart's crusaders in the late 12th century) were recruited from the capture of Messina on. There were also many Greeks in the far south of the Italian mainland, who may also have served.

Following the conquest of Sicily, large numbers of Saracen troops were employed. Most were foot bowmen, others were armed with a mixture of javelins, swords, knives, axes and maces. Some wore light armour. Some, at least, were "splendidly uniformed".

Saracen Close Fighter

ITALO-NORMAN STARTER ARMY 1100 AD		
Commander-in-Chief	1	Field Commander
Sub-commanders	2	2 x Troop Commander
Feudal knights and sergeants	3 BGs	Each comprising 4 bases of feudal knights and sergeants: Superior, Armoured, Undrilled Knights – Lancers, Swordsmen
Saracen archers	4 BGs	Each comprising 6 bases of Saracen archers: Average, Unprotected, Undrilled Light Foot – Bow
Spearmen	1 BG	6 bases of spearmen: Average, Protected, Undrilled Heavy Foot – Defensive Spearmen
Saracen close fighters	1 BG	6 bases of Saracen close fighters: Average, Armoured, Undrilled Medium Foot – Light Spear, Swordsmen
Greeks	1 BG	6 bases of Greeks: Average, Protected, Undrilled Medium Foot – Light Spear, Swordsmen
Camp	1	Unfortified camp
Total	10 BGs	Camp, 12 mounted bases, 42 foot bases, 3 commanders

BUILDING A CUSTOMISED LIST USING OUR ARMY POINTS

Choose an army based on the maxima and minima in the list below. The following special instructions apply to this army:

- Commanders should be depicted as knights.
- Knights and sergeants can always dismount as Armoured, Superior, Undrilled Heavy Foot – Offensive Spearmen.
- The minimum marked * only applies from 1091.

ITALO-NORMAN

Territory Types: Agricultural, Developed, Hilly

C-in-C	Inspired Commander/Field Commander/Troop Commander			80/50/35	1	
Sub-commanders	Field Commander			50	0–2	
	Troop Commander			35	0–3	

Troop name		Troop Type				Capabilities		Points per base	Bases per BG	Total bases
		Type	Armour	Quality	Training	Shooting	Close Combat			
Core Troops										
Feudal knights and sergeants		Knights	Armoured	Superior	Undrilled	–	Lancers, Swordsmen	20	4–6	6–24
Saracen archers	Only from 1072	Light Foot	Unprotected	Average	Drilled or Undrilled	Bow	–	5	6–8	*16–36
		Medium Foot	Protected	Average	Drilled	Bow	–	7	6–8	
			Protected		Undrilled			6		
			Unprotected		Drilled			6		
			Unprotected		Undrilled			5		
Optional Troops										
Italian Communal knights and sergeants		Knights	Armoured	Average	Undrilled	–	Lancers, Swordsmen	16	4–6	0–8
Mercenary knights and sergeants		Knights	Armoured	Superior	Undrilled	–	Lancers, Swordsmen	20	4–6	
Spearmen		Heavy Foot	Protected	Average	Undrilled	–	Defensive Spearmen	6	6–8	0–24
				Average	Drilled			7		
				Poor	Undrilled			4		
				Poor	Drilled			5		
Greeks	Only from 1061	Medium Foot	Protected	Average	Undrilled	–	Light Spear, Swordsmen	6	6–8	0–16
		Light Foot	Unprotected	Average	Undrilled	Javelins	Light Spear	4	6–8	
Saracen cavalry	Only from 1072	Cavalry	Armoured	Average	Drilled	–	Lancers, Swordsmen	13	4	0–4
					Undrilled			12		
Saracen close fighters	Only from 1072	Medium Foot	Armoured	Average	Drilled	–	Light Spear, Swordsmen	9	6–8	0–8
			Armoured		Undrilled			8		
			Protected		Drilled			7		
			Protected		Undrilled			6		
Other foot archers		Light Foot	Unprotected	Average	Undrilled or Drilled	Bow	–	5	6–8	0–12
		Medium Foot	Unprotected	Average	Undrilled	Bow	–	5	6–8	
					Drilled			6		
Crossbowmen		Light Foot	Unprotected	Average	Undrilled or Drilled	Crossbow	–	5	6–8	0–8
		Medium Foot	Protected	Average	Undrilled	Crossbow	–	6	6–8	
					Drilled			7		
Peasants		Mob	Unprotected	Poor	Undrilled	–	–	2	8–12	0–12
Allies										
Lombard allies (Only before 1053) – Field of Glory Companion 8: *Wolves from the Sea: The Dark Ages*										
Sicilian Aghlabid allies (Only in 1061) – Early North African Dynasties – Field of Glory Companion 7: *Decline and Fall: Byzantium at War*										

ITALO–NORMAN ALLIES

Allied commander				Field Commander/Troop Commander			40/25	1	
Troop name		**Troop Type**				**Capabilities**	**Points per base**	**Bases per BG**	**Total bases**
		Type	Armour	Quality	Training	Shooting	Close Combat			
Feudal knights and sergeants		Knights	Armoured	Superior	Undrilled	–	Lancers, Swordsmen	20	4–6	4–8
Saracen archers	Only from 1072	Light Foot	Unprotected	Average	Drilled or Undrilled	Bow	–	5	6–8	*6–12
		Medium Foot	Protected	Average	Drilled	Bow	–	7	6–8	
			Protected		Undrilled			6		
			Unprotected		Drilled			6		
			Unprotected		Undrilled			5		
Spearmen		Heavy Foot	Protected	Average	Undrilled	–	Defensive Spearmen	6	6–8	0–8
				Average	Drilled			7		
				Poor	Undrilled			4		
				Poor	Drilled			5		
Greeks	Only from 1061	Medium Foot	Protected	Average	Undrilled	–	Light Spear, Swordsmen	6	4–6	0–6
		Light Foot	Unprotected	Average	Undrilled	Javelins	Light Spear	4	4–6	
Other foot archers		Light Foot	Unprotected	Average	Undrilled or Drilled	Bow	–	5	4	0–4
		Medium Foot	Unprotected	Average	Undrilled	Bow	–	5	4	
					Drilled			6		

Italo-Norman raiders, by Angus McBride. Taken from Men-at-Arms 376: Italian Medieval Armies 1000–1300

FEUDAL FRENCH

This list covers the armies of Capetian France from 1050 to 1300 AD. During this period the power of the King of France was often overshadowed by that of his nominal vassals. Following the Norman conquest of England in 1066, The Duke of Normandy was now also King of England – thus an equal of the King of France, though still theoretically owing homage for Normandy. Following the coronation of Henry II as King of England in 1154, the situation became even worse. Inheriting Normandy as a possession of the English Crown and Anjou from his father, Henry married France's divorced ex-queen, Eleanor of Aquitaine, and made the Duke of Brittany his vassal, thus ruling most of western France. However, by the end of the reign of King John of England, especially after the French victory over John's Imperialist allies at Bouvines in 1214, King Philip II of France was able to bring most of this territory back under French suzerainty. The English king was left holding only Gascony in the south-west.

The early 13th century also saw the Albigensian Crusade (1209–1229) against the Cathar heretics in Languedoc. In 1213 King Pere of Aragon was in overall command of the army, which included a large Catalano-Aragonese contingent.

King Louis IX (Saint Louis) reigned from 1226 to 1270. He led two crusades, the Seventh Crusade in 1248 which ended in disaster in Egypt, and the Eighth Crusade which petered out after Louis died en route at Tunis in 1270. His son and successor Philip III (the Bold) died in 1285 on the Aragonese Crusade. This had been declared by the Pope following Pere III of Aragon's conquest of Sicily from Philip's uncle Charles of Anjou in the War of the Sicilian Vespers. (see p.94). Philip's son and successor Philip IV (the Fair) reigned until his death in 1314. From 1286 he was also King of Navarre by virtue of his marriage to Juana I of Navarre. He fought wars with Edward I of England in Gascony from 1294–1298 and 1300–1303. By the Treaty of Paris (1303), Philip's daughter Isabella was promised to Edward, the Prince of Wales. This marriage was ultimately to lead to the Hundred Years War, resulting as it did in an English heir to the French throne.

TROOP NOTES

Contemporary illustrations suggest that infantry were armed with heavy cutting weapons and swords as often as spears. However it is likely that they fought in mixed bodies as described in the Catalan list. We treat such mixed bodies as Spearmen.

French Knight

Simon de Montfort, by *Angus McBride*. Taken from *Men-at-Arms 231:*
French Medieval Armies 1000–1300

FEUDAL FRENCH STARTER ARMY 1225 AD

Commander-in-Chief	1	Troop Commander
Sub-commanders	2	2 x Troop Commander
Feudal knights	3 BGs	Each comprising 4 bases of feudal knights: Superior, Heavily Armoured, Undrilled Knights – Lancers, Swordsmen
Mounted crossbowmen	1 BG	4 bases of mounted crossbowmen: Average, Armoured, Undrilled Cavalry – Crossbow, Swordsmen
Feudal spearmen	2 BGs	Each comprising 6 bases of feudal spearmen: Average, Protected, Undrilled Heavy Foot – Defensive Spearmen
Crossbowmen	1 BG	8 bases of crossbowmen: Average, Protected, Undrilled Medium Foot – Crossbow
Archers	1 BG	6 bases of archers: Average, Unprotected, Undrilled Light Foot – Bow
Breton javelinmen	1 BG	4 bases of Breton javelinmen: Average, Unprotected, Undrilled Light Foot – Javelins, Light Spear
Camp	1	Unfortified camp
Total	9 BGs	Camp, 16 mounted bases, 30 foot bases, 3 commanders

BUILDING A CUSTOMISED LIST USING OUR ARMY POINTS

Choose an army based on the maxima and minima in the list below. The following special instructions apply to this army:

- Commanders should be depicted as knights.
- French allied commanders' contingents must conform to the Feudal French allies

list below, but the troops in the contingent are deducted from the minima and maxima in the main list.

- The minimum marked * only applies from 1150.

Communal Militia Spearman

FEUDAL FRENCH

Territory Types: Agricultural, Developed, Woodlands

Troop name		Troop Type				Capabilities		Points per base	Bases per BG	Total bases
C-in-C		Inspired Commander/Field Commander/Troop Commander						80/50/35	1	
Sub-commanders		Field Commander						50	0–2	
		Troop Commander						35	0–3	
French allied commanders		Field Commander/Troop Commander						40/25	0–2	
		Type	Armour	Quality	Training	Shooting	Close Combat			
Core Troops										
Knights and sergeants	Only before 1150	Knights	Armoured	Superior	Undrilled	–	Lancers, Swordsmen	20	4–6	6–32
	Only from 1150	Knights	Heavily Armoured	Superior	Undrilled	–	Lancers, Swordsmen	23	4–6	
Feudal spearmen		Heavy Foot	Protected	Average	Undrilled	–	Defensive Spearmen	6	6–8	0–24
Mercenary spearmen		Heavy Foot	Armoured	Average	Drilled	–	Defensive Spearmen	9	6–8	0–8
			Protected					7		
Communal militia spearmen		Heavy Foot	Protected	Poor	Drilled	–	Defensive Spearmen	5	6–8	0–24
Crossbowmen		Medium Foot	Protected	Average	Undrilled	Crossbow	–	6	6–8	*6–8

Optional Troops										
Separately deployed sergeants	Only from 1150	Cavalry	Armoured	Average	Undrilled	–	Lancers, Swordsmen	12	4–6	0–6
Mounted crossbowmen	Only from 1150	Cavalry	Armoured	Average	Undrilled	Crossbow	Swordsmen	13	4	0–4
Mercenary knights and sergeants	Only before 1150	Knights	Armoured	Superior	Undrilled	–	Lancers, Swordsmen	20	4–6	0–6
	Only from 1150	Knights	Heavily Armoured	Superior	Undrilled	–	Lancers, Swordsmen	23	4–6	
	Only from 1200	Knights	Heavily Armoured	Average	Drilled	–	Lancers, Swordsmen	21	4–6	
Archers	Only before 1150	Light Foot	Unprotected	Average	Undrilled	Bow	–	5	6–8	0–16
	Only from 1150									0–8
Genoese mercenary crossbowmen	Only from 1150	Medium Foot	Protected	Average	Drilled	Crossbow	–	7	6–8	0–8
Low Countries spearmen		Heavy Foot	Armoured	Average	Drilled	–	Offensive Spearmen	10	6–8	0–8
			Armoured	Poor				8		
			Protected	Average				8		
			Protected	Poor				6		
Gascon or Breton javelinmen		Light Foot	Unprotected	Average	Undrilled	Javelins	Light Spear	4	4–6	0–6
Infantry with mixed weapons		Medium Foot	Protected	Average	Undrilled	–	Swordsmen	6	6–8	0–8
Ribauds and peasants		Mob	Unprotected	Poor	Undrilled	–	–	2	8–12	0–12
Allies										
Catalan allies (Only from 1070 to 1213) – Feudal Catalan and Early Crown of Aragon										
Navarrese allies (Only from 1234) – Feudal Navarrese and Aragonese										
Special Campaigns										
Only Albigensian Crusade in 1213										
Catalano–Aragonese knights		Knights	Heavily Armoured	Superior	Undrilled	–	Lancers, Swordsmen	23	4–6	0–8
No Genoese, Gascons or Bretons can be used.										

FEUDAL FRENCH ALLIES

Allied commander		Field Commander/Troop Commander						40/25	1		
Troop name		Troop Type				Capabilities		Points per base	Bases per BG	Total bases	
		Type	Armour	Quality	Training	Shooting	Close Combat				
Knights and sergeants	Only before 1150	Knights	Armoured	Superior	Undrilled	–	Lancers, Swordsmen	20	4–6	4–10	
	Only from 1150	Knights	Heavily Armoured	Superior	Undrilled	–	Lancers, Swordsmen	23	4–6		
Feudal spearmen		Heavy Foot	Protected	Average	Undrilled	–	Defensive Spearmen	6	6–8	0–8	0–12
Communal militia spearmen		Heavy Foot	Protected	Poor	Drilled	–	Defensive Spearmen	5	6–8	0–8	
Crossbowmen		Medium Foot	Protected	Average	Undrilled	Crossbow	–	6	4	0–4	0–6
Archers	Only before 1150	Light Foot	Unprotected	Average	Undrilled	Bow	–	5	4–6	0–6	

Albigensian rebels with French royal knight captive, by Angus McBride. Taken from Men-at-Arms 231:
French Medieval Armies 1000–1300

IMPERIAL GERMAN

This list covers the armies of the German Kings/Emperors, those of the more powerful free cities, the first city leagues (Hanseatic League, Wendian Alliance, Ladbergener City League) and ecclesiastical armies, from 1050 to 1340.

It is in this period that the German Empire started to use the name most connected with it – the Holy Roman Empire. In reality it was never more than an alliance of more or less independent states that were just as likely to squabble among themselves as with outsiders. Only a few strong Emperors proved capable to exerting enough control over the various states to make the construct resemble anything like a true empire. The most famous of these is Friedrich I "Barbarossa".

In 1039 Heinrich III inherited a comparatively well organised and stable empire from his father. When he died unexpectedly in 1056 he was succeeded by his 6-year-old son Heinrich IV, whose mother Agnes ruled in his stead until his 15th birthday. Her weak rule caused a rapid deterioration in Imperial power, including the loss of the Imperial prerogative of appointing the Pope, and the consequent election of a strong Pope opposed to the imperial right of appointment of senior churchmen.

This paved the road to the Investiture Controversy and war with the Pope. Heinrich V, after forcing his father to abdicate, continued the dispute. When agreement was reached in 1122 (Concordat of Worms), the result was a largely independent church, weakening the position of the Emperors. After Heinrich V's death in 1125, Lothar III was elected the new German king, starting the sometimes bitter Welfen–Staufer rivalry.

In 1138 Konrad III became the first Staufer King. He was succeeded in 1152 by Friedrich I "Barbarossa", whose rule started a period of previously unknown prosperity. He emancipated the Empire from the Pope and tried to re-establish the Imperial hold on upper Italy, but was ultimately forced to find a non-military solution. While generally favourable, the agreements made clearly fell short of Barbarossa's ambitions. In 1188 Barbarossa took the cross in the Third Crusade and one year later set out with the largest army any single ruler had ever taken on a crusade. He captured the capital of the Seljuk Sultanate of Rum, but died before he could reach the Holy Land.

His second son Heinrich VI then became King in 1191 and tried to seize Norman lower Italy and Sicily, but did not succeed until 1194. After his early death, his son Friedrich II was declared King, but as he was only 2 years old his claims were ignored, and in 1198 two opposing Kings were elected and fought over the crown until 1208.

In 1212 Friedrich II travelled to Germany from Sicily to claim his right to the throne. He managed to overcome all resistance by 1215. He mainly attempted to create a powerful Kingdom of Sicily, causing him a lot of problems with the Papacy, who felt the Papal state endangered by this. This led to Friedrich being excommunicated several times and even declared as deposed in 1245. In 1228 he went on crusade, despite being excommunicated at the time, and managed to take Jerusalem from the Egyptian Sultan, Al-Kamil, without shedding a single drop of Muslim blood. This only served to infuriate the Pope even more.

In Italy Friedrich II tried to bring the north Italian cities under his control like his predecessors and, like them, enjoyed only very limited success. In order to keep the electors in far away Germany happy Friedrich II granted them many privileges, which in the long run weakened Imperial power considerably.

After his death in 1250, his son Konrad IV, who had already been German King since 1237, also inherited the titles of King of Sicily and Jerusalem. The struggle with the Pope continued, however, and he was never crowned Emperor. After having been defeated by the Papal sponsored anti-king William in 1251, Konrad decided to invade Italy. He proved unable to overcome the Pope's supporters and died of malaria in 1254. After his death, his brother Manfred and later his son Konradin, continued the struggle with the Papacy without much success.

In Germany, Konrad's death vacated the throne, yet none of the claimants were able to achieve universal acceptance. Thus the interregnum began. During the interregnum several kings and anti-kings fought each other, wrecking the Empire's economy until in 1273 Rudolph I of Habsburg was elected king. Imperial influence in Burgundy had all but vanished as a result of French expansion and upper Italy had emancipated itself once more. The decline was partly reversed only after Heinrich VII had come to the throne in 1308. He was also the first German King to be crowned Emperor since Friedrich II.

It was common for Imperial armies to include feudal contingents (usually from the personal holdings of the Emperor) as well as ecclesiastical and city contingents. Feudal contingents from other princes of the empire did occur but were not usual, as most of them were not interested in a strong emperor and had no obligations to send troops, unlike the princes of the church. Troops from the free cities of the empire were usually not required to serve more then half a day's march away from the city. Nevertheless cities sometimes provided troops for campaigns of the Emperor (often mainly mercenary in nature), being granted various privileges in return. The Emperor, the princes of the church and the large cities all made liberal use of mercenaries.

TROOP NOTES

Ministeriales were originally "unfree" milites who held no land in their own right, and could be granted (or even sold) by one lord to another. Their status gradually rose, however, so that by the mid-13th century they were effectively part of the feudal nobility. Moreover, even in the earlier period, there is no evidence to suggest that their performance differed from that of the feudal nobility. The number of ministeriales vastly increased in the Staufer period, partly because the 'princes of the church' could no longer be relied upon due to the Investiture Controversy and partly because more manpower was needed for the Italian wars.

Imperial ministeriales were in effect all ministeriales 'belonging' to the Emperor. We use the term here to single out those ministeriales who were kept together by the Staufer Kings and Emperors as sort of a standing force. As a permanent, paid force that demonstrated both discipline and effectiveness they are classed as Drilled. They were usually supplemented by feudal knights

Ministerialis

and other ministeriales. For longer campaigns (e.g. in Italy) these were paid to serve longer than the customary 40 days. Paid feudal knights and ministeriales may have developed an esprit de corps and increased discipline as well over time, so can be included amongst the imperial ministeriales.

Mercenary knights only emerged significantly during the 13th century, being comparatively rare earlier. There is little evidence to suggest that they were more controlled or less capable in battle than 'noble knights' in this period – most were actually nobles themselves.

Konstaflers were urban knights, rich burghers and their followers. While generally well equipped they were rarely willing to take any risks.

Sources of infantry included sergeants, mercenaries, the militia of smaller towns and cities as well as the Heerbann, the general levy of all able-bodied freemen. The latter was still of some military value in this period, particularly in Saxony, Thuringia and Bavaria.

Fußknechte were followers armed with a miscellany of weapons, mostly short spears, morningstars, warflails, clubs and swords. We treat this mixture as equivalent to Swordsmen capability.

Brabanzonen and Geldoni were mercenaries originally from Brabant and Geldern, but soon picked up recruits from everywhere. While most mercenaries had a reputation for savagery and cruelty, the terms Brabanzonen or Geldoni are used frequently for mercenary bands of unusual aggressiveness and ferocity and/or those which were ill-disciplined.

Hanse Marines were mercenaries employed by the Hanse cities mainly to be used in naval combat. They could also be deployed on land however. While they are described as well trained and equipped we assume that they were not used to operating in large bodies, hence class them as Undrilled. Also it seems likely that they used smaller shields, as customary for ship to ship battles. The armoured option is provided under the assumption that they may have used larger shields while fighting on land.

IMPERIAL GERMAN STARTER ARMY 1225 AD		
Commander-in-Chief	1	Field Commander
Sub-commanders	2	2 x Troop Commander
Imperial ministeriales	1 BG	4 bases of Imperial ministeriales: Superior, Heavily Armoured, Drilled Knights – Lancers, Swordsmen
Other knights and sergeants	1 BG	4 bases of knights and sergeants: Superior, Heavily Armoured, Undrilled Knights – Lancers, Swordsmen
Mounted crossbowmen	1 BG	4 bases of mounted crossbowmen: Average, Armoured, Undrilled Cavalry – Crossbow, Swordsmen
Brabanzonen	1 BG	6 bases of Brabanzonen: Superior, Armoured, Undrilled Heavy Foot – Offensive Spearmen
Feudal or militia spearmen	2 BGs	Each comprising 6 bases of feudal or militia spearmen: Average, Protected, Undrilled Heavy Foot – Defensive Spearmen
Feudal or militia crossbowmen	1 BG	8 bases of feudal or militia crossbowmen: Average, Protected, Undrilled Medium Foot – Crossbow
Archers	1 BG	8 bases of archers: Average, Unprotected, Undrilled Light Foot – Bow
Camp	1	Unfortified camp
Total	8 BGs	Camp, 12 mounted bases, 34 foot bases, 3 commanders

Ministerialis and retinue, by Graham Turner. Taken from Men-at-Arms 310:
German Medieval Armies 1000–1300

BUILDING A CUSTOMISED LIST USING OUR ARMY POINTS

Choose an army based on the maxima and minima in the list below. The following special instructions apply to this army:

- Commanders should be depicted as knights.
- Knights can always dismount as Superior or Average (as mounted type), Armoured or Heavily Armoured (as mounted type), Undrilled or Drilled (as mounted type), Heavy Foot – Heavy Weapon.
- Hanse Marines cannot be used with Free Canton or Hungarian allies.

- Free Canton troops, separately deployed sergeants and Low Country spearmen cannot be used with Hungarian allies.
- Brabanzonen, Geldoni and similar mercenaries cannot be used with Hungarian or Polish allies.
- The minimum marked * only applies from 1150.
- Free Canton, Italian or Hungarian allies cannot be used together.

Fußknechte

IMPERIAL GERMAN

Territory Types: Agricultural, Developed, Hilly, Woodland

C-in-C		Inspired Commander/Field Commander/Troop Commander			80/50/35	1		
Sub-commanders		Field Commander			50	0–2		
		Troop Commander			35	0–3		

Troop name		Troop Type				Capabilities		Points per base	Bases per BG	Total bases	
		Type	Armour	Quality	Training	Shooting	Impact				
Core Troops											
Ministeriales, or feudal knights and sergeants	Only before 1150	Knights	Armoured	Superior	Undrilled	–	Lancers, Swordsmen	20	4–6	0–32	
	Only from 1150	Knights	Heavily Armoured	Superior	Undrilled	–	Lancers, Swordsmen	23	4–6		
Mercenary knights and sergeants	Only before 1150	Knights	Armoured	Superior	Undrilled	–	Lancers, Swordsmen	20	4–6	0–6	4–32
	Only from 1150 to 1199	Knights	Heavily Armoured	Superior	Undrilled	–	Lancers, Swordsmen	23	4–6	0–6	
	Only from 1200	Knights	Heavily Armoured	Superior	Undrilled	–	Lancers, Swordsmen	23	4–6	0–18	
		Knights	Heavily Armoured	Average	Drilled	–	Lancers, Swordsmen	21	4–6		
Konstaflers	Only from 1200	Knights	Heavily Armoured	Average	Undrilled	–	Swordsmen	17	4–6	0–6	
Mercenary or good quality militia spearmen		Heavy Foot	Armoured	Average	Drilled	–	Defensive Spearmen	9	6–8	Before 1150 0–8, From 1150 0–12	8–48
					Undrilled			8			
Feudal or militia spearmen		Heavy Foot	Protected	Average	Drilled	–	Defensive Spearmen	7	6–10	6–48	
				Average	Undrilled			6			
				Poor	Drilled			5			
				Poor	Undrilled			4			
Low Countries spearmen		Heavy Foot	Armoured	Average	Drilled	–	Offensive Spearmen	10	6–10	0–20	
			Armoured	Poor				8			
			Protected	Average				8			
			Protected	Poor				6			
Mercenary or good quality militia Crossbowmen		Medium Foot	Protected	Average	Drilled	Crossbow	–	7	6–8	0–12	
					Undrilled			6			
Feudal or militia crossbowmen		Medium Foot	Protected	Average	Undrilled	Crossbow	–	6	6–8	*6–18	
			Protected	Poor	Drilled			5			
			Protected	Poor	Undrilled			4			
			Unprotected	Average	Undrilled			5			
			Unprotected	Poor	Undrilled			3			
		Light Foot	Unprotected	Average	Undrilled	Crossbow	–	5	6–8	6–24	
				Poor				3			
Archers		Medium Foot	Protected	Average	Drilled	Bow	–	7	6–8	0–8	
			Protected	Average	Undrilled			6			
			Unprotected	Average	Drilled			6			
			Unprotected	Average	Undrilled			5			
			Unprotected	Poor	Undrilled			3			
		Light Foot	Unprotected	Average	Undrilled	Bow	–	5	6–8		
				Poor				3			

Optional Troops											
Imperial *ministeriales*	Only from 1152 to 1254	Knights	Heavily Armoured	Superior	Drilled	–	Lancers, Swordsmen	26	4–6	0–6	0–6
Teutonic knights	Only from 1226	Knights	Heavily Armoured	Superior	Drilled	–	Lancers, Swordsmen	26	4	0–4	
Mounted crossbowmen	Only from 1150	Cavalry	Armoured	Average	Drilled	Crossbow	Swordsmen	14	4–6	0–6	
					Undrilled			13			
Separately deployed sergeants	Only from 1150	Cavalry	Armoured	Average	Undrilled	–	Lancers, Swordsmen	12	4–6	0–6	
Brabanzonen, Geldoni and similar mercenaries	Only from 1150	Heavy Foot	Armoured	Superior	Undrilled	–	Offensive Spearmen	12	4–6	0–6	
				Average				9			
Hanse marines	Only from 1250	Medium Foot	Protected	Average	Undrilled	–	Light Spear, Swordsmen	6	4–6		
			Armoured					8			
Fußknechte		Heavy Foot or Medium Foot	Protected	Average	Undrilled	–	Swordsmen	6	6–8	0–8	
Fortified camp								24		0–1	

Allies
Free Canton allies (Only from 1106) – Early Medieval Frisian or other Free Canton Allies
German City allies
German Ecclesiastical allies
German Feudal allies
Hungarian allies (Only in 1278) – Early Hungarian

Special Campaigns										
Only Imperial German armies in Italy										
Italian Contadini knights and sergeants	Only before 1150	Knights	Armoured	Superior	Undrilled	–	Lancers, Swordsmen	20	4	0–4
	Only from 1150 to 1199	Knights	Heavily Armoured	Superior	Undrilled	–	Lancers, Swordsmen	23	4	
	Only from 1200	Knights	Heavily Armoured	Average	Undrilled	–	Lancers, Swordsmen	18	4	
Italian Communal knights and sergeants	Only from 1100 to 1149	Knights	Armoured	Average	Undrilled	–	Lancers, Swordsmen	16	4	0–4
	Only from 1150	Knights	Heavily Armoured	Average	Undrilled	–	Lancers, Swordsmen	18	4	
Italian town militia spearmen		Heavy Foot	Protected	Average	Drilled	–	Defensive Spearmen	7	6–8	0–8
				Poor				5		
Italian contadini spearmen		Heavy Foot	Protected	Poor	Undrilled	–	Defensive Spearmen	4	6–8	0–8
Swabian schwertknechte	Only from 1154 to 1235	Heavy Foot	Armoured	Average	Undrilled	–	Heavy Weapon	9	4–6	0–6
Italian Communal allies										
Italian Feudal allies										

No Teutonic knights, Konstaflers, Hanse Marines, Brabanzonen, Geldoni and similar mercenaries can be used. No allies except German Feudal, Italian Communal or Italian Feudal can be used. Foot minima do not apply to the main army nor to German Feudal allies.

GERMAN CITY ALLIES

Allied commander		Field Commander/Troop Commander					40/25	1	
Troop name		**Troop Type**				**Capabilities**	**Points per base**	**Bases per BG**	**Total bases**
		Type	Armour	Quality	Training	Shooting	Impact			

Troop name		Type	Armour	Quality	Training	Shooting	Impact	Points per base	Bases per BG	Total bases	
Mercenary knights and sergeants	Only before 1150	Knights	Armoured	Superior	Undrilled	–	Lancers, Swordsmen	20	4	0–4	0–8
	Only from 1150	Knights	Heavily Armoured	Superior	Undrilled	–	Lancers, Swordsmen	23	4	0–4	
	Only from 1200	Knights	Heavily Armoured	Average	Drilled	–	Lancers, Swordsmen	21	4	0–4	
Konstaflers	Only from 1200	Knights	Heavily Armoured	Average	Undrilled	–	Swordsmen	17	4	0–4	
Mercenary or good quality militia spearmen	Only from 1150	Heavy Foot	Armoured	Average	Drilled	–	Defensive Spearmen	9	4–6	0–6	8–24
					Undrilled			8			
Militia spearmen		Heavy Foot	Protected	Average	Drilled	–	Defensive Spearmen	7	6–10	8–24	
				Average	Undrilled			6			
				Poor	Drilled			5			
				Poor	Undrilled			4			
Mercenary or good quality militia crossbowmen		Medium Foot	Protected	Average	Drilled	Crossbow	–	7	4–6	0–6	*6–12
					Undrilled			6			
Militia crossbowmen		Medium Foot	Protected	Average	Undrilled	Crossbow	–	6	6–8	*6–12	
			Protected	Poor	Drilled			5			
			Protected	Poor	Undrilled			4			
			Unprotected	Average	Undrilled			5			
			Unprotected	Poor	Undrilled			3			
Archers	Only before 1200	Medium Foot	Protected	Average	Drilled	Bow	–	7	4–6	0–6	
			Protected	Average	Undrilled			6			
			Unprotected	Average	Drilled			6			
			Unprotected	Average	Undrilled			5			
			Unprotected	Poor	Undrilled			3			

GERMAN ECCLESIASTICAL ALLIES

Allied commander		Field Commander/Troop Commander					40/25		1	
Troop name		**Troop Type**				**Capabilities**		**Points per base**	**Bases per BG**	**Total bases**
		Type	Armour	Quality	Training	Shooting	Impact			
Ministeriales, or feudal knights and sergeants	Only before 1150	Knights	Armoured	Superior	Undrilled	–	Lancers, Swordsmen	20	4–6	4–8
	Only from 1150	Knights	Heavily Armoured	Superior	Undrilled	–	Lancers, Swordsmen	23	4–6	0–8
Mercenary knights and sergeants	Only before 1150	Knights	Armoured	Superior	Undrilled	–	Lancers, Swordsmen	20	4	0–4
	Only from 1150 to 1199	Knights	Heavily Armoured	Superior	Undrilled	–	Lancers, Swordsmen	23	4	0–4
	Only from 1200	Knights	Heavily Armoured	Superior	Undrilled	–	Lancers, Swordsmen	23	4	0–8
		Knights	Heavily Armoured	Average	Drilled	–	Lancers, Swordsmen	21	4	
Mercenary spearmen		Heavy Foot	Protected	Average	Drilled	–	Defensive Spearmen	7	6–8	Before 1150 6–8, From 1150 6–12
					Undrilled			6		
		Heavy Foot	Armoured	Average	Drilled	–	Defensive Spearmen	9	6	0–6
					Undrilled			8		
Mercenary crossbowmen		Medium Foot	Protected	Average	Drilled	Crossbow	–	7	4–6	0–6
					Undrilled			6		
Other crossbowmen		Medium Foot	Protected	Average	Undrilled	Crossbow	–	6	6–8	*6–12
			Unprotected	Average				5		
			Unprotected	Poor				3		
Archers		Medium Foot	Protected	Average	Drilled	Bow	–	7	4–6	0–6
			Protected	Average	Undrilled			6		
			Unprotected	Average	Drilled			6		
			Unprotected	Average	Undrilled			5		
			Unprotected	Poor	Undrilled			3		

(Total bases, right column further span: 4–8 for Mercenary knights and sergeants; 6–12 for Mercenary spearmen; *6–12 for the crossbowmen group)

FEUDAL GERMAN

This list covers the armies of the major autonomous states and dynasties that constituted the 'German Empire' from 1050 to 1340. The various regional lords bore a multitude of titles, usually Herzog (Duke), Erzherzog (Archduke), or König (King), the actual title not really telling anything about their real power, especially since many held several such titles. Over time they became known collectively as Kurfürsten (Electors) or 'Princes of the Empire' indicating that they had the privilege to elect, from among

themselves, the next German King if the throne was vacant.

Feudalism in the strict sense of the word never took root in large parts of Germany. It was stronger in the western and central parts, especially the Rhineland, somewhat less established in the north, and weakest in the south and east of the Empire. In many regions the rulers still kept large bands of followers as personal retinues rather then as vassals. The introduction of ministeriales in the 11th century

only served to further slow the spread of feudalism in Germany.

Unlike the princes of the church, the lay princes were not obliged to provide troops to the Emperor, and few did so unless they gained something in return. This left them largely free to do as they pleased with their often considerable armies and, accordingly, throughout the period the princes were just as likely, and often more likely, to quarrel among themselves (and of course with the free cities of the Empire and sometimes the princes of the church) than with outsiders. Such battles, however, were usually comparatively small affairs using only a fraction of the full force each side could call on in an emergency. As time went on the legal code became more complex so the more powerful lords sometimes used lesser, officially independent, nobles as proxies to carry out their battles for them, so as to avoid legal problems. As far as battles with external powers are concerned these were mostly with Denmark, Poland, Hungary and France, but again there were only very few major field battles.

During the time of the Staufer Emperors, some of the princes used the lack of Imperial attention to slowly expand their territory into Slavic areas, sometimes by force, but usually by peaceful colonization. Thus Silesia and Pomeria were added to the Empire.

The largest battles and campaigns fought by the princes during this period were usually the result of two alliances electing opposing kings. This was especially true during the interregnum that lasted from 1254–1273 and

Mercenary Knight

saw sometimes not just two but several 'German Kings' at once.

For most of this period the armies of the princes were more 'feudal' in nature (compared to the more mercenary based armies of the Emperor, the ecclesiastical lords and the independent cities) bolstered by troops from the unfree cities in their realms and mercenaries. Many of the bigger cities had the privilege of not being required to send troops further then half a day's march from the city. The smaller cities and towns usually were not so lucky. Ecclesiastical allies were common, alliances with the independent cities much rarer but they did occur from time to time.

The use of mercenaries increased during the interregnum, partly due to the extensive campaigns fought and partly because there were now suddenly lots of mercenaries available, who had previously served the Staufer Emperors in Italy and were now looking for new employment opportunities.

TROOP NOTES

Ministeriales were originally "unfree" milites who held no land in their own right, and could be granted (or even sold) by one lord to another. Their status gradually rose, however, so that by the mid-13th century they were effectively part of the feudal nobility. Moreover, even in the earlier period, there is no evidence to suggest that their performance differed from that of the feudal nobility.

Mercenary knights only emerged significantly during the 13th century, being comparatively rare earlier. There is little evidence to suggest that they were more controlled or less capable in battle than 'noble knights' in this period – most were actually nobles themselves.

Fußknechte were followers armed with a miscellany of weapons, mostly short spears,

German knight and auxiliaries, by Graham Turner. Taken from Men-at-Arms 310: German Medieval Armies 1000–1300

morningstars, warflails, clubs and swords. We treat this mixture as equivalent to Swordsmen capability.

Swabian and Bavarian Schwertknechte were paid the same as mounted sergeants, but seem to have fought only on foot using two handed swords.

Brabanzonen and Geldoni were mercenaries originally from Brabant and Geldern, but soon picked up recruits from everywhere. While most mercenaries had a reputation for savagery and cruelty, the terms Brabanzonen or Geldoni are used frequently for mercenary bands of unusual aggressiveness and ferocity and/or those which were ill-disciplined.

Amongst the feudal infantry we include sergeants, the militia of smaller towns and cities, and also the Heerbann, the general levy of all able-bodied freemen. The latter was still of some military value in this period, particularly in Saxony, Thuringia and Bavaria.

FEUDAL GERMAN STARTER ARMY 1225 AD		
Commander-in-Chief	1	Troop Commander
Sub-commanders	2	2 x Troop Commander
Knights and sergeants	2 BGs	Each comprising 4 bases of knights and sergeants: Superior, Heavily Armoured, Undrilled Knights – Lancers, Swordsmen
Hungarians	2 BGs	Each comprising 4 bases of Hungarians: Average, Unprotected, Undrilled Light Horse – Bow
Swabian or Bavarian schwertknechte	1 BG	6 bases of Swabian or Bavarian schwertknechte: Average, Armoured, Undrilled Heavy Foot – Heavy Weapon
Feudal spearmen	2 BGs	Each comprising 6 bases of feudal spearmen: Average, Protected, Undrilled Heavy Foot – Defensive Spearmen
Feudal crossbowmen	1 BG	8 bases of feudal crossbowmen: Average, Protected, Undrilled Medium Foot – Crossbow
Archers	1 BG	6 bases of archers: Average, Protected, Undrilled Medium Foot – Bow
Fußknechte	1 BG	6 bases of Fußknechte: Average, Protected, Undrilled Medium Foot – Swordsmen
Camp	1	Unfortified camp
Total	10 BGs	Camp, 16 mounted bases, 38 foot bases, 3 commanders

BUILDING A CUSTOMISED LIST USING OUR ARMY POINTS

Choose an army based on the maxima and minima in the list below. The following special instructions apply to this army:

- Commanders should be depicted as knights.
- Knights can always dismount as Superior or Average (as mounted type), Armoured or Heavily Armoured (as mounted type), Undrilled or Drilled (as mounted type), Heavy Foot – Heavy Weapon.
- Fußknechte can be graded as Heavy Foot or Medium Foot but all must be graded the same.
- Feudal German allied commanders' contingents must conform to the German Feudal allies list below, but the troops in the contingent are deducted from the minima and maxima in the main list.
- The minimum marked * only applies from 1150.

- Danish and Polish allies cannot be used together.
- Optional troops from the South and East Germany section cannot be used with optional troops from the North, Central and West Germany section, nor with Danish or Polish Allies. For the purpose of this list East and South Germany includes roughly:

Bohemia, Silesia, Swabia, Bavaria, Carinthia, Moravia, Styria and Austria (based on the borders around 1250).

Mounted Crossbowman

FEUDAL GERMAN

Territory Types: Agricultural, Developed, Hilly, Woodland

C-in-C	Inspired Commander/Field Commander/Troop Commander						80/50/35		1	
Sub-commanders	Field Commander						50		0–2	
	Troop Commander						35		0–3	
Feudal German allied commanders	Field Commander/Troop Commander						40/25		0–2	

Troop name		Troop Type				Capabilities		Points per base	Bases per BG	Total bases	
		Type	Armour	Quality	Training	Shooting	Impact				
Core Troops											
Ministeriales, or feudal knights and sergeants	Only before 1150	Knights	Armoured	Superior	Undrilled	–	Lancers, Swordsmen	20	4–6	6–32	
	Only from 1150	Knights	Heavily Armoured	Superior	Undrilled	–	Lancers, Swordsmen	23	4–6		
Mercenary knights and sergeants	Only before 1150	Knights	Armoured	Superior	Undrilled	–	Lancers, Swordsmen	20	4–6	0–6	6–32
	Only from 1150 to 1199	Knights	Heavily Armoured	Superior	Undrilled	–	Lancers, Swordsmen	23	4–6	0–6	
	Only from 1200	Knights	Heavily Armoured	Superior	Undrilled	–	Lancers, Swordsmen	23	4–6	0–18	
		Knights	Heavily Armoured	Average	Drilled	–	Lancers, Swordsmen	21	4–6		
Mercenary spears or foot sergeants		Heavy Foot	Protected	Average	Drilled	–	Defensive Spearmen	7	6–8	0–8	8–40
			Protected		Undrilled			6			
			Armoured		Drilled			10			
			Armoured		Undrilled			9			
Feudal spearmen		Heavy Foot	Protected	Average	Undrilled	–	Defensive Spearmen	6	6–8	0–32	
				Poor				4			
Mercenary crossbowmen		Medium Foot	Protected	Average	Drilled	Crossbow	–	7	6–8	0–12	
					Undrilled			6			
Feudal crossbowmen		Medium Foot	Protected	Average	Undrilled	Crossbow	–	6	6–8	*6–18	6–24
			Unprotected	Average				5			
			Unprotected	Poor				3			
		Light Foot	Unprotected	Average	Undrilled	Crossbow	–	5	6–8		
				Poor				3			
Archers		Medium Foot	Protected	Average	Undrilled	Bow	–	6	6–8	0–8	
			Protected	Poor				4			
			Unprotected	Average				5			
			Unprotected	Poor				3			
		Light Foot	Unprotected	Average	Undrilled	Bow	–	5	6–8		
				Poor				3			

Optional Troops										
Mounted crossbowmen	Only from 1200	Cavalry	Armoured	Average	Undrilled	Crossbow	Swordsmen	13	4–6	0–6
Fußknechte		Heavy Foot or Medium Foot	Protected	Average	Undrilled	–	Swordsmen	6	6–8	0–12
Fortified camp								24		0–1
Only South and East Germany										
Hungarians	Only from 1150	Light Horse	Unprotected	Average	Undrilled	Bow	–	8	4–6	0–8
		Light Horse	Unprotected	Average	Undrilled	Bow	Swordsmen	10	4–6	
Swabian or Bavarian schwertknechte		Heavy Foot	Armoured	Average	Undrilled	–	Heavy Weapon	9	4–6	0–6
Slav foot		Medium Foot	Protected	Average	Undrilled	–	Light Spear	5	6–8	0–24
				Poor				3		
Only North, Central and West Germany										
Free Canton spearmen	Only from 1106	Medium Foot	Protected	Average	Undrilled	–	Offensive Spearmen	7	6–8	0–12
			Unprotected					6		
Brabanzonen, Geldoni or similar mercenaries	Only from 1150	Heavy Foot	Armoured	Superior	Undrilled	–	Offensive Spearmen	12	4–6	0–6
				Average				9		
Separately deployed sergeants		Cavalry	Armoured	Average	Undrilled	–	Lancers, Swordsmen	12	4–6	0–6
Allies										
Danish allies – Viking or Post-Viking Scandinavian										
German allies – German Ecclesiastical or German City allies										
Polish allies – Feudal Polish										
Special Campaigns										
Only Konradin at Tagliacozzo in 1268										
Italian, Sicilian and Castilian knights		Knights	Heavily Armoured	Superior	Undrilled	–	Lancers, Swordsmen	23	4–6	8–20
Castilian jinetes		Light Horse	Unprotected	Average	Undrilled	Javelins	Light Spear	7	4	0–4
No optional troops or allies can be used. Foot minima do not apply.										

GERMAN FEUDAL ALLIES

Allied commander		Field Commander/Troop Commander						40/25		1	
Troop name		**Troop Type**				**Capabilities**		Points per base	Bases per BG	Total bases	
		Type	Armour	Quality	Training	Shooting	Impact				
Ministeriales, or feudal knights and sergeants	Only before 1150	Knights	Armoured	Superior	Undrilled	–	Lancers, Swordsmen	20	4–6	4–8	4–10
	Only from 1150	Knights	Heavily Armoured	Superior	Undrilled	–	Lancers, Swordsmen	23	4–6		
Mercenary knights and sergeants	Only from 1200	Knights	Heavily Armoured	Superior	Undrilled	–	Lancers, Swordsmen	23	4–6	0–6	
		Knights	Heavily Armoured	Average	Drilled	–	Lancers, Swordsmen	21	4–6		
Feudal spearmen		Heavy Foot	Protected	Average	Undrilled	–	Defensive Spearmen	6	6–8	6–12	
				Poor				4			
Mercenary crossbowmen		Medium Foot	Protected	Average	Drilled	Crossbow	–	7	4	0–4	4–8
					Undrilled			6			
Feudal crossbowmen		Medium Foot	Protected	Average	Undrilled	Crossbow	–	6	4–6	0–6	
			Unprotected	Average	Undrilled			5			
			Unprotected	Poor				3			
Fußknechte		Heavy Foot or Medium Foot	Protected	Average	Undrilled	–	Swordsmen	6	4	0–4	
Only South and East Germany											
Slav foot		Medium Foot	Protected	Average	Undrilled	–	Light Spear	5	6–8	0–8	
				Poor				3			

COMMUNAL ITALIAN

This list covers Italian Communal armies from 1050 to 1320 AD.

This is the period during which the urban Italian republics (communes) established their autonomy. They did so by playing off the Pope against the Holy Roman Emperor. During the various disputes between these major powers, the Italian communes preserved their effective independence by supporting either the Pope or the Emperor. Those supporting the Pope came to be known as "Guelfs", while those supporting the Emperor came to be known as "Ghibellines", although these terms were not in common use until the mid-13th century. Guelf cities were mainly those where control by the Emperor was the greater threat, whereas Ghibelline cities tended to be those in areas close to the Papal States. However, smaller towns often protected their own independence by adopting the opposite party to their larger neighbours. Even within the cities there were often Guelf and Ghibelline factions, with one or other faction being in power at various times.

The Lombard League, formed circa 1176, was a Guelf alliance formed to counter the Emperor Friedrich I Barbarossa's ambition to control northern Italy. It included, amongst others, Milan, Piacenza, Cremona, Mantua, Bergamo, Brescia, Bologna, Padua, Treviso, Vicenza, Venice, Verona, Lodi, and Parma. It also included some feudal lords, such as the Marquis Malaspina and Ezzelino da Romano. The League was renewed several times, and was once again successful in countering the Emperor Friedrich II in the second quarter of the 13th century. It was dissolved in 1250 after Friedrich's death.

TROOP NOTES

Contadini were troops supplied by the rural districts surrounding the Italian towns.

Most "mercenary" knights in Communal armies prior to the first half of the 13th century were in fact Communal knights from other towns. They are included in the total of Communal knights.

Carroccios were wagons carrying a rectangular platform on which were placed the standard of city and an altar. Guarded by the bravest soldiers, they acted as rallying-points and as the repository of the city's honour – their loss being regarded as a humiliating calamity. They are best represented as part of the army's camp.

Carroccio

Northern Italian militia, by Angus McBride. Taken from Men-at-Arms 376: Italian Medieval Armies 1000–1300

ITALIAN COMMUNAL STARTER ARMY 1225 AD		
Commander-in-Chief	1	Field Commander
Sub-commanders	2	2 x Troop Commander
Mercenary knights and sergeants	1 BG	4 bases of mercenary knights and sergeants: Superior, Heavily Armoured, Undrilled Knights – Lancers, Swordsmen
Communal knights and sergeants	1 BG	6 bases of Communal knights and sergeants: Average, Heavily Armoured, Undrilled Knights – Lancers, Swordsmen
Mounted crossbowmen	1 BG	4 bases of mounted crossbowmen: Average, Unprotected, Drilled Light Horse – Crossbow
Town militia spearmen	3 BGs	Each comprising 8 bases of town militia spearmen: Average, Protected, Drilled Heavy Foot – Defensive Spearmen
Contadini spearmen	1 BG	6 bases of Contadini spearmen: Poor, Protected, Undrilled Heavy Foot – Defensive Spearmen
Crossbowmen	1 BG	6 bases of crossbowmen: Average, Unprotected, Drilled Light Foot – Crossbow
Archers	1 BG	6 bases of archers: Average, Unprotected, Drilled Light Foot – Bow
Camp	1	Unfortified camp
Total	9 BGs	Camp, 14 mounted bases, 42 foot bases, 3 commanders

BUILDING A CUSTOMISED LIST USING OUR ARMY POINTS

Choose an army based on the maxima and minima in the list below. The following special instructions apply to this army:

Crossbowmen

- Commanders should be depicted as knights.

COMMUNAL ITALIAN

Territory Types: Agricultural, Developed, Hilly

C-in-C	Inspired Commander/Field Commander/Troop Commander					80/50/35		1	
Sub-commanders	Field Commander					50		0–2	
	Troop Commander					35		0–3	

Troop name		Troop Type				Capabilities		Points per base	Bases per BG	Total bases	
		Type	Armour	Quality	Training	Shooting	Close Combat				
Core Troops											
Contadini knights and sergeants	Only before 1150	Knights	Armoured	Superior	Undrilled	–	Lancers, Swordsmen	20	4–6	0–8	4–32
	Only from 1150 to 1199	Knights	Heavily Armoured	Superior	Undrilled	–	Lancers, Swordsmen	23	4–6		
	Only from 1200	Knights	Heavily Armoured	Average	Undrilled	–	Lancers, Swordsmen	18	4–6		
Communal knights and sergeants	Only from 1100 to 1149	Knights	Armoured	Average	Undrilled	–	Lancers, Swordsmen	16	4–6	4–12	
	Only from 1150	Knights	Heavily Armoured	Average	Undrilled	–	Lancers, Swordsmen	18	4–6		
Mercenary knights and sergeants	Only from 1200	Knights	Heavily Armoured	Superior	Undrilled	–	Lancers, Swordsmen	23	4–6	0–12	
		Knights	Heavily Armoured	Average	Drilled	–	Lancers, Swordsmen	21	4–6		
Town militia spearmen		Heavy Foot	Protected	Average	Drilled	–	Defensive Spearmen	7	6–8	12–48	18–96
		Heavy Foot	Protected	Poor		–	Defensive Spearmen	5			
Mercenary or good quality town militia spearmen	Any date	Heavy Foot	Protected	Average	Drilled	–	Defensive Spearmen	7	6–8	0–12	
	Only from 1150	Heavy Foot	Armoured	Average	Drilled	–	Defensive Spearmen	9	6–8		
Contadini spearmen		Heavy Foot	Protected	Poor	Undrilled	–	Defensive Spearmen	4	6–8	6–48	
Crossbowmen	Any date	Light Foot	Unprotected	Average	Drilled	Crossbow	–	5	6–8		6–24
		Medium Foot	Protected	Average	Drilled	Crossbow	–	7	6–8		
		Medium Foot	Protected	Poor				5			
Pavisiers and crossbowmen	Only from 1200	Heavy Foot	Protected	Average	Drilled	–	Defensive Spearmen	7	1/2	6	
		Medium Foot	Protected	Average	Drilled	Crossbow	–	7	1/2		
		Heavy Foot	Protected	Poor	Drilled	–	Defensive Spearmen	5	1/2	6	
		Medium Foot	Protected	Poor	Drilled	Crossbow	–	5	1/2		
Carroccio, its defenders, and supply camp		Fortified Camp						24		0–1	

Optional Troops										
Mounted crossbowmen	Only from 1200	Cavalry	Armoured	Average	Drilled	Crossbow	Swordsmen	14	4	0–4
		Light Horse	Unprotected	Average	Drilled	Crossbow	–	7	4	
Foot archers		Light Foot	Unprotected	Average	Drilled	Bow	–	5	6–8	0–8
Axemen		Heavy Foot	Protected	Average	Drilled	–	Heavy Weapon	8	4–6	0–6
Javelinmen	Only from 1200	Medium Foot	Protected	Average	Drilled	–	Light Spear	6	6–8	0–16
Allies										
Italian Communal allies – up to 2 contingents										
Italian Feudal allies										

ITALIAN COMMUNAL ALLIES

Allied commander		Field Commander/Troop Commander						40/25		1	
Troop name		Troop Type				Capabilities		Points per base	Bases per BG	Total bases	
		Type	Armour	Quality	Training	Shooting	Close Combat				
Contadini knights and sergeants	Only before 1150	Knights	Armoured	Superior	Undrilled	–	Lancers, Swordsmen	20	4–6	0–4	
	Only from 1150 to 1199	Knights	Heavily Armoured	Superior	Undrilled	–	Lancers, Swordsmen	23	4–6		
	Only from 1200	Knights	Heavily Armoured	Average	Undrilled	–	Lancers, Swordsmen	18	4–6		
Communal knights and sergeants	Only from 1100 to 1149	Knights	Armoured	Average	Undrilled	–	Lancers, Swordsmen	16	4	0–4	0–8
	Only from 1150	Knights	Heavily Armoured	Average	Undrilled	–	Lancers, Swordsmen	18	4		
Mercenary knights and sergeants	Only from 1200	Knights	Heavily Armoured	Superior	Undrilled	–	Lancers, Swordsmen	23	4	0–4	
		Knights	Heavily Armoured	Average	Drilled	–	Lancers, Swordsmen	21	4		
Town militia spearmen		Heavy Foot	Protected	Average	Drilled	–	Defensive Spearmen	7	6–8	6–12	6–24
				Poor				5			
Contadini spearmen		Heavy Foot	Protected	Poor	Undrilled	–	Defensive Spearmen	4	6–8	0–12	
Crossbowmen	Any date	Light Foot	Unprotected	Average	Drilled	Crossbow	–	5	6–8	0–8	
		Medium Foot	Protected	Average	Drilled	Crossbow	–	7	6–8		
				Poor				5			
Pavisiers and crossbowmen	Only from 1200	Heavy Foot	Protected	Average	Drilled	–	Defensive Spearmen	7	1/2	6	
		Medium Foot	Protected	Average	Drilled	Crossbow	–	7	1/2		
		Heavy Foot	Protected	Poor	Drilled	–	Defensive Spearmen	5	1/2	6	
		Medium Foot	Protected	Poor	Drilled	Crossbow	–	5	1/2		
Javelinmen	Only from 1200	Medium Foot	Protected	Average	Drilled	–	Light Spear	6	4–6	0–6	

ITALIAN FEUDAL ALLIES

Allied commander		Field Commander/Troop Commander						40/25	1	
Troop name		**Troop Type**				**Capabilities**		**Points per base**	**Bases per BG**	**Total bases**
		Type	Armour	Quality	Training	Shooting	Close Combat			
Feudal knights and sergeants	Only before 1150	Knights	Armoured	Superior	Undrilled	–	Lancers, Swordsmen	20	4	4–8
	Only from 1150	Knights	Heavily Armoured	Superior	Undrilled	–	Lancers, Swordsmen	23	4	
Mercenary knights and sergeants	Only before 1150	Knights	Armoured	Superior	Undrilled	–	Lancers, Swordsmen	20	4	4–8
	Only from 1150	Knights	Heavily Armoured	Superior	Undrilled	–	Lancers, Swordsmen	23	4	0–4
	Only from 1200	Knights	Heavily Armoured	Average	Drilled	–	Lancers, Swordsmen	21	4	
Scutiferi	Only before 1200	Light Horse	Unprotected	Average	Undrilled	Javelins	Light Spear	7	4–6	4–6
Feudal spearmen		Heavy Foot	Protected	Average	Undrilled	–	Defensive Spearmen	6	6–8	6–24
				Poor				4		
Crossbowmen		Light Foot	Unprotected	Average	Undrilled	Crossbow	–	5	4–6	0–6
		Medium Foot	Protected	Average	Undrilled	Crossbow	–	6	4–6	
				Poor				4		

The Battle of Campaldino, by Christa Hook. Taken from *Warrior 25: Italian Militiaman 1260–1392*

PAPAL ITALIAN

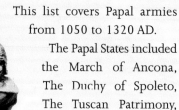

This list covers Papal armies from 1050 to 1320 AD.

The Papal States included the March of Ancona, The Duchy of Spoleto, The Tuscan Patrimony, Campagna, Marittima and Romagna, governed by officials called rectors. A substantial number

Town Militia Spearman

of feudal knights were available from these territories. More reliance, however, was placed on the town militias, although requests to the communes for troops were often ignored or met by the supply of only token contingents. Some of the communes within the Papal States, such as Forli in Romagna, consistently adopted a Ghibelline stance (see p.51) to resist Papal control. Increasing numbers of mercenaries were also employed. If all else failed, the Pope could call a Crusade – and this was done several times against rebellious cities as well as external enemies.

PAPAL STARTER ARMY 1225 AD		
Commander-in-Chief	1	Field Commander
Sub-commanders	2	2 x Troop Commander
Feudal and mercenary knights and sergeants	3 BGs	Each comprising 4 bases of knights and sergeants: Superior, Heavily Armoured, Undrilled Knights – Lancers, Swordsmen
Mounted crossbowmen	1 BG	4 bases of mounted crossbowmen: Average, Unprotected, Undrilled Light Horse – Crossbow
Town militia spearmen	2 BGs	Each comprising 8 bases of town militia spearmen: Average, Protected, Drilled Heavy Foot – Defensive Spearmen
Crossbowmen	1 BG	6 bases of crossbowmen: Average, Unprotected, Undrilled Light Foot – Crossbow
Archers	1 BG	6 bases of archers: Average, Unprotected, Undrilled Light Foot – Bow
Camp	1	Unfortified camp
Total	8 BGs	Camp, 16 mounted bases, 28 foot bases, 3 commanders

BUILDING A CUSTOMISED LIST USING OUR ARMY POINTS

Choose an army based on the maxima and minima in the list below. The following special instructions apply to this army:

• Commanders should be depicted as knights.

Crossbowman

PAPAL ITALIAN

PAPAL ITALIAN									
Territory Types: Agricultural, Developed, Hilly									
C-in-C	Inspired Commander/Field Commander/Troop Commander						80/50/35	1	
Sub-commanders	Field Commander						50	0–2	
	Troop Commander						35	0–3	
Troop name	Troop Type				Capabilities		Points per base	Bases per BG	Total bases
	Type	Armour	Quality	Training	Shooting	Close Combat			
Core Troops									
Feudal knights and sergeants	Only before 1150	Knights	Armoured	Superior	Undrilled	—	Lancers, Swordsmen	20	4–6	0–8
	Only from 1150	Knights	Heavily Armoured	Superior	Undrilled	—	Lancers, Swordsmen	23	4–6	
Mercenary knights and sergeants	Only before 1150	Knights	Armoured	Superior	Undrilled	—	Lancers, Swordsmen	20	4–6	0–8
	Only from 1150 to 1199	Knights	Heavily Armoured	Superior	Undrilled	—	Lancers, Swordsmen	23	4–6	0–8
	Only from 1200	Knights	Heavily Armoured	Superior	Undrilled	—	Lancers, Swordsmen	23	4–6	0–12
		Knights	Heavily Armoured	Average	Drilled	—	Lancers, Swordsmen	21	4–6	
Town militia spearmen		Heavy Foot	Protected	Average	Drilled	—	Defensive Spearmen	7	6–8	0–16
				Poor		—		5		
Mercenary or good quality town militia spearmen	Any date	Heavy Foot	Protected	Average	Drilled	—	Defensive Spearmen	7	6–8	0–12
	Only from 1150	Heavy Foot	Armoured	Average	Drilled	—	Defensive Spearmen	9	6–8	
Feudal spearmen		Heavy Foot	Protected	Average	Undrilled	—	Defensive Spearmen	6	6–8	0–8
				Poor		—		4		
Crossbowmen	Any date	Light Foot	Unprotected	Average	Drilled	Crossbow	—	5	6–8	
		Medium Foot	Protected	Average	Drilled	Crossbow	—	7	6–8	
				Poor		Crossbow	—	5		
Pavisiers and crossbowmen	Only from 1200	Heavy Foot	Protected	Average	Drilled	—	Defensive Spearmen	7	1/2	6	6–18
		Medium Foot	Protected	Average	Drilled	Crossbow	—	7	1/2	
		Heavy Foot	Protected	Poor	Drilled	—	Defensive Spearmen	5	1/2	6
		Medium Foot	Protected	Poor	Drilled	Crossbow	—	5	1/2	
Optional Troops									
Mounted crossbowmen	Only from 1200	Cavalry	Armoured	Average	Drilled	Crossbow	Swordsmen	14	4	0–4
		Light Horse	Unprotected	Average	Drilled	Crossbow	—	7	4	
Foot archers		Light Foot	Unprotected	Average	Drilled	Bow	—	5	6–8	0–8
Javelinmen	Only from 1200	Medium Foot	Protected	Average	Drilled	—	Light Spear	6	6–8	0–16
Allies									
Byzantine allies (Only before 1072) – Nikephorian Byzantine – See Field of Glory Companion 7: Decline and Fall: Byzantium at War									
Italian Communal allies – up to 2 contingents									
Italian Feudal allies									
Lombard allies (Only before 1072) – Lombard – See Field of Glory Companion 7: Decline and Fall: Byzantium at War									
Norman allies (Only before 1151) – Italo-Norman									

The 8–36 total for militia spearmen spans Mercenary or good quality town militia spearmen and related rows. The 6–20 total spans the Mercenary knights and sergeants rows.

EARLY SCOTS ISLES AND HIGHLANDS

This list covers the armies of the Scots Isles and Highlands from 1050 until 1300.

At the start of this period the Isles and much of the Highlands were under the control of the Norwegian Earl of Orkney. Norsemen and Scottish Gaels came to share a common culture. Internecine strife between rival heirs to the earldom, however, meant that the Earldom was often divided between rival claimants. By the mid-12th century the Isle of Man and the Hebrides were independent, being united by Somerled in 1158 as the Kingdom of Mann and the Isles. Somerled's descendants became Clan MacDougall, which held most of Argyll and the Isles of Mull, Lismore, Jura, Tiree and Coll until the beginning of the 14th century when they lost most of their territory after opposing King Robert the Bruce, and Clan MacDonald, Lords of the Isles until the title was suppressed by King James IV of Scotland in 1493.

Highlander

Following the Battle of Largs in 1263, in which a Scottish army, assisted by stormy weather, prevented a Norwegian fleet from landing troops in force, the Norwegians abandoned their attempts to control the Western Isles. Angus Mor MacDonald accepted King Alexander III of Scotland as his (nominal) overlord. By the Treaty of Perth in 1266 Magnus VI of Norway formally ceded the Western Isles to Scotland. Norway retained control over Orkney until 1468, though the Earls were Scotsmen from 1232.

TROOP NOTES

The commonest weapon of the Islesman was the two-handed axe, but the Lewis chessmen (c.1175) and a proportion of later grave effigies show spear and sword instead. Later battle accounts suggest that the wealthier Highlanders were equipped with mail, bow, targe, sword and/or axe. Lesser followers, equipped only with targe, sword or knife made up the rear ranks.

EARLY SCOTS ISLES AND HIGHLANDS STARTER ARMY 1225 AD		
Commander-in-Chief	1	Troop Commander
Sub-commanders	2	2 x Troop Commander
Islesmen	3 BGs	Each comprising 8 bases of Islesmen: Average, Protected, Undrilled Heavy Foot – Offensive Spearmen
Islesmen	2 BGs	Each comprising 8 bases of Islesmen: Average, Protected, Undrilled Heavy Foot – Heavy Weapon
Highlanders	3 BGs	Each comprising 8 bases of Highlanders: Average, Protected, Undrilled Medium Foot – Bow*, Impact Foot, Swordsmen
Scouts	1 BG	4 bases of scouts: Average, Unprotected, Undrilled Light Foot – Bow
Camp	1	Unfortified camp
Total	9 BGs	Camp, 68 foot bases, 3 commanders

Troops of the Kingdom of the Isles, by Angus McBride. Taken from Men-at-Arms 396: Medieval
Scandinavian Armies (1): 1100–1300

BUILDING A CUSTOMISED LIST USING OUR ARMY POINTS

Choose an army based on the maxima and minima in the list below. The following special instructions apply to this army:

- Commanders should be depicted as Islesmen or Highlanders.

Islesmen

EARLY SCOTS ISLES AND HIGHLANDS

Territory Types: Hilly, Mountains

C-in-C	Inspired Commander/Field Commander/Troop Commander						80/50/35		1
Sub-commanders	Field Commander						50		0–2
	Troop Commander						35		0–3
Troop name	**Troop Type**				**Capabilities**		**Points per base**	**Bases per BG**	**Total bases**
	Type	Armour	Quality	Training	Shooting	Close Combat			
Core Troops									
Islesmen	Heavy Foot	Protected	Average	Undrilled	–	Heavy Weapon	7	6–8	32–108
	Heavy Foot	Protected	Average	Undrilled	–	Offensive Spearmen	7	6–8	
Highlanders	Medium Foot	Protected	Average	Undrilled	Bow*	Impact Foot, Swordsmen	8	6–8	0–48
Scouts	Light Foot	Unprotected	Average	Undrilled	Bow	–	5	4	0–4
Irish mercenaries	Medium Foot	Unprotected	Average	Undrilled	–	Heavy Weapon	6	6–8	0–16
	Medium Foot	Unprotected	Average	Undrilled	–	Light Spear, Swordsmen	5	6–8	
Allies									
Galwegian allies (Only before 1161) – Galwegian									
Viking allies (Only before 1266) – See Field of Glory Companion 8: *Wolves from the Sea: The Dark Ages*									

EARLY SCOTS ISLES AND HIGHLANDS ALLIES

Allied commander	Field Commander/Troop Commander						40/25		1
Troop name	**Troop Type**				**Capabilities**		**Points per base**	**Bases per BG**	**Total bases**
	Type	Armour	Quality	Training	Shooting	Close Combat			
Islesmen	Heavy Foot	Protected	Average	Undrilled	–	Heavy Weapon	7	6–8	0–24
	Heavy Foot	Protected	Average	Undrilled	–	Offensive Spearmen	7	6–8	
Highlanders	Medium Foot	Protected	Average	Undrilled	Bow*	Impact Foot, Swordsmen	8	6–8	0–16

FEUDAL SCOTS

This list covers lowland Scots armies from 1052 to 1300.

In the second quarter of the 12th century King David I of Scotland supported the claim of his niece the Empress Matilda against King Stephen of England. He invaded northern England several times. In 1138 a pitched battle was fought at Northallerton against a local English force. The Scots were defeated with heavy losses.

Over the rest of the period Scots forces entered England on a number of occasions. However, the main task of the Scottish Kings was to expand their control, which initially was confined to the lowlands, over the rest of Scotland. It was not until 1266 that King Magnus VI of Norway ceded the Western Isles to Scotland, and Orkney remained under Norwegian control until 1468.

Following the death of King Alexander III in 1286, there was no direct male heir to the throne. Alexander's granddaughter Margaret (daughter of King Eirik II of Norway) died on the way from Norway to take the throne. Following a six year interregnum, King John Balliol was crowned, with the support of King Edward I

Spearman

of England, in November 1292. His rival, Robert Bruce of Annandale, grandfather of Robert the Bruce, accepted this with reluctance. Over the following years Edward of England sought to use the concessions he had won in return for his support to undermine the authority of King John and the independence of Scotland. In 1295 King John made an alliance with the King of France. In 1296 Edward invaded, and deposed King John. In 1297 William Wallace and Andrew de Moray raised the country against the English, winning a victory at Stirling Bridge. In 1298, however, Edward came north in person and defeated Wallace at Falkirk. Wallace was later captured in 1305 and executed.

In 1306 Robert the Bruce, who had alternately supported the English and Scottish sides since 1292, declared himself King of Scots and was crowned at Scone. There followed many years of war before Robert decisively defeated Edward II's army at Bannockburn in 1314. Nevertheless, it took until 1328 to secure recognition by Edward III of Scotland's independence with Robert as its king.

TROOP NOTES

Scottish knightly armour development largely kept pace with English, though we allow for the possibility of a slight lag.

The "common army" made up the bulk of Scottish forces, comprising poorly equipped peasant infantry armed with 3.7 metre (12 foot) spears, usually unarmoured with only helmet and shield.

William Wallace at Stirling Bridge, by Angus McBride. Taken from Campaign 117: Stirling Bridge &
Falkirk 1297–98

FEUDAL SCOTS STARTER ARMY 1225 AD

Commander-in-Chief	1	Field Commander
Sub-commanders	2	2 x Troop Commander
Knights and sergeants	1 BG	4 bases of knights and sergeants: Superior, Heavily Armoured, Undrilled Knights – Lancers, Swordsmen
Spearmen	6 BGs	Each comprising 8 bases of spearmen: Average, Protected, Undrilled Heavy Foot – Offensive Spearmen
Archers	1 BG	8 bases of archers: Average, Unprotected, Undrilled Light Foot – Bow
Ribauds	1 BG	6 bases of ribauds: Poor, Unprotected, Undrilled Medium Foot – no capabilities
Camp	1	Unfortified camp
Total	9 BGs	Camp, 4 mounted bases, 62 foot bases, 3 commanders

BUILDING A CUSTOMISED LIST USING OUR ARMY POINTS

Choose an army based on the maxima and minima in the list below. The following special instructions apply to this army:

- Commanders should be depicted as knights.
- Knights and sergeants can always dismount as Superior, Armoured or Heavily Armoured (as mounted type), Undrilled Heavy Foot – Offensive Spearmen.

Archer

FEUDAL SCOTS

Territory Types: Agricultural, Hilly, Woodlands

Troop name		Troop Type				Capabilities		Points per base	Bases per BG	Total bases
		Type	Armour	Quality	Training	Shooting	Close Combat			
C-in-C		Inspired Commander/Field Commander/Troop Commander						80/50/35	1	
Sub-commanders		Field Commander						50	0–2	
		Troop Commander						35	0–3	
Core Troops										
Knights and sergeants	Only before 1200	Knights	Armoured	Superior	Undrilled	–	Lancers, Swordsmen	20	4–6	0–8
				Average				16		
	Only from 1150	Knights	Heavily Armoured	Superior	Undrilled	–	Lancers, Swordsmen	23	4–6	
				Average				18		
Spearmen		Heavy Foot	Protected	Average	Undrilled	–	Offensive Spearmen	7	6–10	32–142
			Unprotected					6		
Archers		Light Foot	Unprotected	Average	Undrilled	Bow	–	5	6–8	0–12
				Poor				3		
		Medium Foot	Unprotected	Average	Undrilled	Bow	–	5		
				Poor				3		
Optional Troops										
Ribaulds		Medium Foot	Unprotected	Poor	Undrilled	–	–	2	6	0–6
Pits or other traps		Field Fortifications						3		0–16
Fortified camp								24		0–1
Allies										
Galwegian allies (Only before 1162) – Galwegian										
Isles and/or Highland allies – Early Scots Isles and Highlands										

FEUDAL SCOTS ALLIES										
Allied commander		Field Commander/Troop Commander						40/25	1	
Troop name		Troop Type				Capabilities		Points per base	Bases per BG	Total bases
		Type	Armour	Quality	Training	Shooting	Close Combat			
Knights and sergeants	Only before 1200	Knights	Armoured	Superior	Undrilled	–	Lancers, Swordsmen	20	4	0–4
				Average				16		
	Only from 1150	Knights	Heavily Armoured	Superior	Undrilled	–	Lancers, Swordsmen	23	4	
				Average				18		
Spearmen		Heavy Foot	Protected	Average	Undrilled	–	Offensive Spearmen	7	6–10	8–32
			Unprotected					6		
Archers		Light Foot	Unprotected	Average	Undrilled	Bow	–	5	4	0–4
				Poor				3		
		Medium Foot	Unprotected	Average	Undrilled	Bow	–	5		
				Poor				3		

GALWEGIAN ALLIES									
Allied commander	Field Commander/Troop Commander						40/25	1	
Troop name	Troop Type				Capabilities		Points per base	Bases per BG	Total bases
	Type	Armour	Quality	Training	Shooting	Close Combat			
Warriors	Medium Foot	Protected	Average	Undrilled	–	Impact Foot, Swordsmen	7	8–12	8–36
		Unprotected					6		

EARLY RUSSIAN

By the mid-11th century, the fusion of Scandinavian and Slavic elements that was Kievan Rus had reached the height of its power under Prince Yaroslav the Wise, ruling over a huge territory comprising modern Belarus, northern Ukraine and western Russia. The senior Rurikid Prince ruled from Kiev, while the other Russian cities were governed by junior princes of the dynasty. To the south, the steppe was dominated by the nomadic Cumans (known to the Russians as Polovtsy). To the west were the kingdoms of Poland and Hungary. At this time, Kievan Rus was not only geographically the largest, but also in several ways one of most cultural advanced states in northern Europe. Literacy was widespread, and Kiev's population was four times that of contemporary London.

As time went on, however, the increasingly numerous princes came to identify more with their local regions than with the larger polity. They fought amongst themselves, often seeking external alliances with the Cumans, Poles or Hungarians. Trade declined after the Crusades, especially the Fourth Crusade, opened up alternative trade routes with the Middle East. By the time of the Mongol invasion, Russia was divided into a number of rival principalities, including the Principalities of Kiev, Vladimir-Suzdal, Chernigov, Halych-Volhynia, Polotsk and Smolensk, and the Republic of Novgorod.

German Mercenary

In 1223 a Russian army, with Cuman allies, was defeated at the Kalka River by a Mongol reconnaissance force. Between 1236 and 1239, Mongol forces subjugated the Volga Bulgars, the Cumans and the Russian principalities. Most of the major Russian cities, including Kiev, were sacked. The south Russian principalities of Kiev and Chernigov were completely subjugated, the others, with the exception of Novgorod, were reduced to vassal status. Novgorod, though independent, had its own problems with aggression by the Swedes and Teutonic Knights. Halych-Volhynia was eventually absorbed into the Polish-Lithuanian Commonwealth.

Alexander Nevsky, as elected Prince of Novgorod, won victories over the Swedes at the Neva in 1240 and the Teutonic Knights at Lake Peipus in 1242 – though both of these "battles" may in fact have been more in the nature of skirmishes, and their importance subsequently exaggerated for propaganda purposes. In 1252 he was installed as Grand Prince of Vladimir, which he remained until his death in 1263.

This list covers Russian armies from 1054 until 1264, by which time we assume that horse archer tactics had been universally adopted under Mongol influence.

TROOP NOTES

The proportion of cavalry steadily increased during this period. The numerous princes and their retinues (druzhina) supplied armoured cavalry. Turkic mercenary horse archers, including Pechenegs and other Turkic nomad tribes, were employed in large numbers and often settled in Russian territory – becoming "our pagans" (svoi poganye).

Town militia (polk) supplied well-equipped spearmen, whose proportion in field armies steadily decreased throughout the period. They also supplied a few relatively poorly equipped cavalry, usually used as scouts. Land-owning peasants (smerdy) were sometimes called up to fight but were of general poor quality, lacking experience or good equipment.

Peasant

EARLY RUSSIAN STARTER ARMY 1225 AD		
Commander-in-Chief	1	Troop Commander
Sub-commanders	2	2 x Troop Commander
Nobles and retainers	3 BGs	Each comprising 4 bases of nobles and retainers: Superior, Armoured, Undrilled Cavalry – Light Spear, Swordsmen
Turkic mercenaries	3 BGs	Each comprising 4 bases of Turkic mercenaries: Average, Unprotected, Undrilled Light Horse – Bow, Swordsmen
Town militia spearmen	2 BGs	Each comprising 8 bases of town militia spearmen: Average, Protected, Undrilled Heavy Foot – Defensive Spearmen
Archers	2 BGs	Each comprising 6 bases of archers: Average, Unprotected, Undrilled Light Foot – Bow
Fortified camp	1	Fortified camp
Total	10 BGs	Fortified Camp, 24 mounted bases, 28 foot bases, 3 commanders

Russian militia, by Angus McBride. Taken from Men-at-Arms 333: Armies of Medieval Russia 750–1250

BUILDING A CUSTOMISED LIST USING OUR ARMY POINTS

Choose an army based on the maxima and minima in the list below. The following special instructions apply to this army:

- Commanders should be depicted as noble cavalry.
- Russian allied commanders' contingents must conform to the Early Russian allies list below, but the troops in the contingent are deducted from the minima and maxima in the main list.
- Germans and Lithuanians cannot be used with each other, nor with Poles or Hungarians.
- The minimum marked * only applies if any foot are used.

EARLY RUSSIAN

Territory Types: Agricultural, Woodlands

C-in-C	Inspired Commander/Field Commander/Troop Commander					80/50/35		1	
Sub-commanders	Field Commander					50		0–2	
	Troop Commander					35		0–3	
Russian allied commanders	Field Commander/Troop Commander					40/25		0–2	

Troop name	Troop Type				Capabilities		Points per base	Bases per BG	Total bases
	Type	Armour	Quality	Training	Shooting	Close Combat			
Core Troops									
Nobles and retainers	Cavalry	Armoured	Superior	Undrilled	–	Light Spear, Swordsmen	16	4–6	12–32
			Average				12		
Town militia spearmen with or without supporting archers	Heavy Foot	Armoured	Average	Undrilled	–	Defensive Spearmen	8	2/3 or all	8–24
		Protected					6		
	Light Foot	Unprotected	Average	Undrilled	Bow	–	5	1/3 or 0	
Peasant spearmen with or without support archers	Heavy Foot	Protected	Poor	Undrilled	–	Defensive Spearmen	4	2/3 or all	8–40
	Light Foot	Unprotected	Poor	Undrilled	Bow	–	3	1/3 or 0	0–9
Separately deployed archers	Light Foot	Unprotected	Average	Undrilled	Bow	–	5	6–8	0–16
			Poor				3		
Turkic mercenaries	Light Horse	Unprotected	Average	Undrilled	Bow	Swordsmen	10	4–6	0–24
	Cavalry	Unprotected	Average	Undrilled	Bow	Swordsmen	10	4–6	
		Protected					11		
Optional Troops									
Town militia cavalry	Light Horse	Unprotected	Average	Undrilled	Javelins	Light Spear	7	4	0–4
German mercenaries	Only before 1150	Knights	Armoured	Superior	Undrilled	–	Lancers, Swordsmen	20	4	0–4
	Only from 1150	Knights	Heavily Armoured	Superior	Undrilled	–	Lancers, Swordsmen	23	4	
	Only from 1200	Knights	Heavily Armoured	Average	Drilled	–	Lancers, Swordsmen	21	4	
Lithuanian cavalry	Light Horse	Unprotected	Average	Undrilled	Javelins	Light Spear, Swordsmen	9	4	0–4
	Cavalry	Unprotected	Average	Undrilled	–	Light Spear, Swordsmen	8	4	
		Protected					9		

Troop name		Type	Armour	Quality	Training	Shooting	Close Combat	Points per base	Bases per BG	Total bases
Polish cavalry	Only before 1200	Cavalry	Armoured	Superior	Undrilled	–	Light Spear, Swordsmen	16	4	
	Only from 1200 to 1241	Knights	Armoured	Superior	Undrilled	–	Lancers, Swordsmen	20	4	0–4
	Only from 1242	Knights	Heavily Armoured	Superior	Undrilled	–	Lancers, Swordsmen	23	4	
Hungarian cavalry		Light Horse	Unprotected	Average	Undrilled	Bow	–	8	4	0–4
		Light Horse	Unprotected	Average	Undrilled	Bow	Swordsmen	10	4	
Poorly equipped peasants		Mob	Unprotected	Poor	Undrilled	–	–	2	8	0–8
Fortified camp								24		0–1
Allies										
Cuman (Polovtsy) allies – Cuman – See Field of Glory Companion 4: *Swords and Scimitars: The Crusades*										
Hungarian allies – Early Hungarian										
Polish allies (Only from 1150) – Feudal Polish										

EARLY RUSSIAN ALLIES

Allied commander		Field Commander/Troop Commander						40/25		1
Troop name		Troop Type				Capabilities		Points per base	Bases per BG	Total bases
		Type	Armour	Quality	Training	Shooting	Close Combat			
Nobles and retainers		Cavalry	Armoured	Superior	Undrilled	–	Light Spear, Swordsmen	16	4–6	4–10
				Average				12		
Town militia spearmen with or without supporting archers		Heavy Foot	Armoured	Average	Undrilled	–	Defensive Spearmen	8	2/3 or all	6–9 *6–9
			Protected					6		
		Light Foot	Unprotected	Average	Undrilled	Bow	–	5	1/3 or 0	0–12
Separately deployed archers		Light Foot	Unprotected	Average	Undrilled	Bow	–	5	4–6	0–6
				Poor				3		
Turkic mercenaries		Light Horse	Unprotected	Average	Undrilled	Bow	Swordsmen	10	4–6	
		Cavalry	Unprotected	Average	Undrilled	Bow	Swordsmen	10	4–6	0–8
			Protected					11		

FEUDAL POLISH

In 966 AD Mieszko I, leader of the Slavic tribe of Polans, accepted Christianity. This marked the creation of the Polish state and the foundation of the Piast dynasty. By the end of his reign he had transformed Poland into one of the strongest states in Eastern Europe. His son Bolesław the Brave continued his work and became the first King of Poland in 1025. A period of instability under Bolesław's son, Mieszko II, was followed by a resurgence under his son, Casimir the Restorer, who reigned till 1058.

Following his death, there was a period of instability until Bolesław III Wrymouth reunited the country in 1106. However, before his death in 1138, he divided up power in the country between his four sons, with the eldest, Władysław, having the title of Grand Duke of Kraków. Władysław's attempt to deprive his brothers of power and reunite the country led to civil war, resulting in Władysław's defeat and exile in 1146. Thereafter the country remained effectively divided, with the Duke of Krakow as titular Duke of Poland, but the other Polish principalities effectively independent. It was not until the early years of the 14th century that much of the country was reunited by King Władysław the Elbow-High.

In 1241 Mongol forces invaded Central Europe. The main force, under the supreme command of the Great Khan's general Subutai, invaded Hungary, while a diversionary force invaded Poland. The Hungarians were severely defeated at Mohi, and the Poles, under Duke Henry II of Silesia, at Legnica (Liegnitz). Fortunately for Europe, the Great Khan, Ögedei, died the same year, and the Mongol leaders broke off the campaign to take part in the election of a new Great Khan.

Polish Nobles

This list covers Polish armies from 1058 until 1300.

TROOP NOTES

The Polish nobility lagged behind Western Europe somewhat in terms of tactics and equipment.

The wealthier infantrymen formed up as heavy spearmen, in leather or padded linen sleeveless armour, sometimes reinforced with leather strips or small iron plates, and with a substantial shield. By the 13th century some wore actual mail, but still only a minority

Peasant foot, sometimes equipped only with clubs, nevertheless also often carried shields. Later in the period the long-handled two-handed axe became popular.

FEUDAL POLISH STARTER ARMY 1275 AD		
Commander-in-Chief	1	Field Commander
Sub-commanders	2	2 x Troop Commander
Noble cavalry	2 BGs	Each comprising 4 bases of noble cavalry: Superior, Heavily Armoured, Undrilled Knights – Lancers, Swordsmen
Russian cavalry	1 BG	4 bases of Russian cavalry: Superior, Armoured, Undrilled Cavalry – Bow, Swordsmen
Lithuanian cavalry	1 BG	4 bases of Lithuanian cavalry: Average, Unprotected, Undrilled Light Horse – Javelins, Light Spear, Swordsmen
Hungarian cavalry	1 BG	4 bases of Hungarian cavalry: Average, Unprotected, Undrilled Light Horse – Bow
Spearmen	2 BGs	Each comprising 8 bases of spearmen: Average, Protected, Undrilled Heavy Foot – Defensive Spearmen
Peasant archers	2 BGs	Each comprising 6 bases of peasant archers: Average, Unprotected, Undrilled Light Foot – Bow
Camp	1	Unfortified camp
Total	9 BGs	Camp, 20 mounted bases, 28 foot bases, 3 commanders

Polish troops, by Gerry Embleton. Taken from Men-at-Arms 445: Medieval Polish Armies 966–1500

BUILDING A CUSTOMISED LIST USING OUR ARMY POINTS

Choose an army based on the maxima and minima in the list below. The following special instructions apply to this army:

- Commanders should be depicted as noble cavalry.
- Polish allied commanders' contingents must conform to the Feudal Polish allies list below, but the troops in the contingent are deducted from the minima and maxima in the main list.
- Hungarian allies cannot be used with German or Teutonic Order allies.

Peasant Axeman

FEUDAL POLISH

Territory Types: Agricultural, Woodlands

C-in-C	Inspired Commander/Field Commander/Troop Commander					80/50/35	1	
Sub-commanders	Field Commander					50	0–2	
	Troop Commander					35	0–3	
Polish allied commanders	Field Commander/Troop Commander					40/25	0–2	

Troop name		Troop Type				Capabilities		Points per base	Bases per BG	Total bases
		Type	Armour	Quality	Training	Shooting	Close Combat			
Core Troops										
Noble cavalry	Only before 1200	Cavalry	Armoured	Superior	Undrilled	–	Light Spear, Swordsmen	16	4–6	6–28
	Only from 1200 to 1241	Knights	Armoured	Superior	Undrilled	–	Lancers, Swordsmen	20	4–6	
	Only from 1242	Knights	Heavily Armoured	Superior	Undrilled	–	Lancers, Swordsmen	23	4–6	
Spearmen		Heavy Foot	Protected	Average	Undrilled	–	Defensive Spearmen	6	6–8	8–48
Peasant archers		Light Foot	Unprotected	Average	Undrilled	Bow	–	5	6–8	8–56
		Medium Foot	Unprotected	Average	Undrilled	Bow	–	5	6–8	
			Protected					6		
Optional Troops										
Lithuanian cavalry	Only from 1242	Light Horse	Unprotected	Average	Undrilled	Javelins	Light Spear, Swordsmen	9	4–6	0–6
		Cavalry	Unprotected	Average	Undrilled	–	Light Spear, Swordsmen	8	4–6	
			Protected					9		
Hungarian or Cuman cavalry	Only from 1242	Light Horse	Unprotected	Average	Undrilled	Bow	–	8	4	0–4
		Light Horse	Unprotected	Average	Undrilled	Bow	Swordsmen	10	4	
Russian cavalry	Only from 1242 to 1264	Cavalry	Armoured	Superior	Undrilled	–	Light Spear, Swordsmen	16	4	0–4
				Average				12		
	Only from 1265	Cavalry	Armoured	Superior	Undrilled	Bow	Swordsmen	18	4	
				Average				14		
Peasant axemen	Only from 1200	Medium Foot	Unprotected	Average	Undrilled	–	Heavy Weapon	6	4–6	0–6
Peasant slingers		Light Foot	Unprotected	Average	Undrilled	Sling	–	4	6–8	0–12
Poorly equipped peasants		Mob	Unprotected	Poor	Undrilled	–	–	2	8–12	0–20
			Protected					3		
Allies										

German allies (Only from 1147 to 1241) – German Feudal

Hungarian allies (Only from 1147 to 1230) – Early Hungarian

Teutonic Order allies (Only from 1224 to 1241) – Early Teutonic Knights

FEUDAL POLISH ALLIES										
Allied commander		Field Commander/Troop Commander						40/25	1	
Troop name		Troop Type				Capabilities		Points per base	Bases per BG	Total bases
		Type	Armour	Quality	Training	Shooting	Close Combat			
Noble cavalry	Only before 1200	Cavalry	Armoured	Superior	Undrilled	–	Light Spear, Swordsmen	16	4–6	4–8
	Only from 1200 to 1241	Knights	Armoured	Superior	Undrilled	–	Lancers, Swordsmen	20	4–6	
	Only from 1242	Knights	Heavily Armoured	Superior	Undrilled	–	Lancers, Swordsmen	23	4–6	
Spearmen		Heavy Foot	Protected	Average	Undrilled	–	Defensive Spearmen	6	6–8	6–16
Peasant archers		Light Foot	Unprotected	Average	Undrilled	Bow	–	5	6–8	6–18
		Medium Foot	Unprotected	Average	Undrilled	Bow	–	5	6–8	
			Protected					6		

ANGLO-NORMAN

This list covers English armies from 1072 to 1154 AD. During this period wars were fought against English and Anglo-Norman rebels, Danes, Scots, Welsh, Bretons and French.

The Norman conquest of England by William I the Conqueror in 1066 replaced the Saxon monarchy with a Norman dynasty. English resistance, with Danish and Scottish support, continued until 1071. In 1079 William's eldest son Robert Curthose rebelled in Normandy, and personally unhorsed William in battle. They were to some extent reconciled the following year. In 1087 William died after a fall from his horse. On his deathbed he divided his succession between Robert Curthose in Normandy and his younger son William II Rufus in England.

An inevitable succession struggle resulted, with William defeating Robert's partisans in England in 1088, and invading Normandy in 1091. After defeating Robert he forced him to cede some of his French lands, though thereafter he supported him against France and the brothers named each other heir presumptive to their respective domains. In 1096 Robert set forth as one of the leaders of the First Crusade, mortgaging Normandy to William to raise funds. He was on his way back in 1100 when William was killed, ostensibly in a hunting accident.

In Robert's absence his youngest brother, Henry I, seized the English throne. In 1101 Robert invaded England, but was outmanoeuvred and forced to renounce his claim to the throne.

In 1105 Henry invaded Normandy, decisively defeating Robert at the Battle of Tinchebrai the following year. Robert spent the remaining 28 years of his life in prison. Henry died in 1135, leaving no male heir. He had named his daughter Matilda as his heir, but the barons instead crowned his nephew Stephen of Blois. Civil war followed, lasting until 1153 when Stephen accepted Matilda's son Henry as his heir. Stephen died in 1154, and was duly succeeded by Henry II.

TROOP NOTES

Infantry were armed with a mixture of axes, swords and spears. As it is probable that they fought in mixed bodies similar to the earlier Viking or Saxon shieldwall, we treat such mixed bodies as Spearmen.

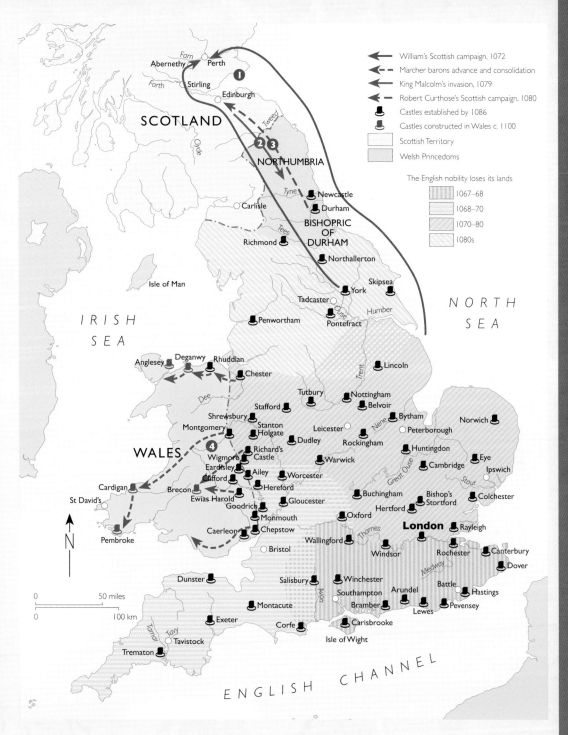

The following legend appears on the map:

- William's Scottish campaign, 1072
- Marcher barons advance and consolidation
- King Malcolm's invasion, 1079
- Robert Curthose's Scottish campaign, 1080
- Castles established by 1086
- Castles constructed in Wales c. 1100
- Scottish Territory
- Welsh Princedoms

The English nobility loses its lands

- 1067–68
- 1068–70
- 1070–80
- 1080s

The securing of Norman control over Britain, 1072–1086. Taken from Essential Histories 12: **Campaigns of the Norman Conquest**

ANGLO–NORMAN STARTER ARMY 1100 AD

Commander-in-Chief	1	Field Commander
Sub-commanders	2	2 x Troop Commander
Knights and sergeants	3 BGs	Each comprising 4 bases of feudal knights and sergeants: Superior, Armoured, Undrilled Knights – Lancers, Swordsmen
Separately deployed sergeants	1 BG	4 bases of separately deployed sergeants: Average, Protected, Undrilled Cavalry – Lancers, Swordsmen
Foot sergeants etc.	3 BGs	Each comprising 8 bases of foot sergeants etc.: Average, Protected, Undrilled Heavy Foot – Defensive Spearmen
Archers	2 BGs	Each comprising 6 bases of archers: Average, Unprotected, Undrilled Light Foot – Bow
Camp	1	Unfortified camp
Total	9 BGs	Camp, 16 mounted bases, 36 foot bases, 3 commanders

BUILDING A CUSTOMISED LIST USING OUR ARMY POINTS

Choose an army based on the maxima and minima in the list below. The following special instructions apply to this army:

- Commanders should be depicted as knights.
- Knights and sergeants can always dismount

as Superior, Armoured, Undrilled Heavy Foot – Offensive Spearmen.

- French allies cannot be used with any Welsh

Dismounted Knight

ANGLO–NORMAN

Territory Types: Agricultural, Woodlands

C-in-C	Inspired Commander/Field Commander/Troop Commander						80/50/35	1	
Sub-commanders	Field Commander						50	0–2	
	Troop Commander						35	0–3	
Troop name	Troop Type				Capabilities		Points per base	Bases per BG	Total bases
	Type	Armour	Quality	Training	Shooting	Close Combat			
Core Troops									
Knights and sergeants	Knights	Armoured	Superior	Undrilled	–	Lancers, Swordsmen	20	4–6	6–26
Foot sergeants, English freemen and town militia	Heavy Foot	Protected	Average	Undrilled	–	Defensive Spearmen	6	6–8	12–60
			Poor				4		
Archers	Light Foot	Unprotected	Average	Undrilled	Bow	–	5	6–8	6–24
	Medium Foot	Unprotected	Average	Undrilled	Bow	–	5	6–8	
Optional Troops									
Separately deployed sergeants or Marcher muntatores	Cavalry	Armoured	Average	Undrilled	–	Lancers, Swordsmen	12	4	0–4
		Protected					9		
Mercenary spearmen	Heavy Foot	Armoured	Average	Drilled	–	Defensive Spearmen	9	6–8	0–8
		Protected					7		
Marcher Welsh foot	Medium Foot	Unprotected	Average	Undrilled	–	Offensive Spearmen	6	6–8	0–8
Allies									
North Welsh allies – Later Welsh									
French allies – Feudal French									

LATER WELSH

At the time of the Norman conquest of England in 1066, the most powerful ruler in Wales was Bleddyn ap Cynfyn, Prince of Gwynedd (in the north-west) and Powys (in the east). Soon afterwards, the Normans began to make incursions into Wales, overrunning Gwent in the south-east by 1070, and reaching Deheubarth in the south-west by 1074. Following the death of Bleddyn ap Cynfyn in 1075, civil war broke out in Wales, allowing the Normans to make inroads into North Wales. Much of Gwynedd was seized in 1081 following the treacherous capture of Gruffydd ap Cynan at a parley. Morgannwg, in the south, was annexed in 1090, Deheubarth in 1093. Welsh fortunes were at a low ebb.

In 1094, however, the Welsh revolted and some of the lost territories were restored to Welsh rule. A strong kingdom of Gwynedd was rebuilt by Gruffydd ap Cynan. The Normans were heavily defeated at Crug Mawr in 1136 and Ceredigion recovered. Powys also remained independent, though it was permanently split from 1160. Most of Deheubarth was reconquered from the Normans by 1171, when Rhys ap Gruffydd (The Lord Rhys) came to terms with Henry II. Rhys also controlled much of the rest of South Wales through client princes. On his death in 1197, his lands were split between his sons, who became clients of the North.

Llywelyn ab Iorwerth, also known as Llywelyn Fawr (The Great), was sole ruler of Gwynedd by 1200 and between then and his death in 1240 gained effective control over much of Wales. A period of internecine strife following his death was followed by the rise of Llywelyn ap Gruffydd, also known as Llywelyn Ein Llyw Olaf (Our Last Leader), who was recognised as "Prince of Wales" by Henry III in the Treaty of Montgomery in 1267.

Edward I invaded Llywelyn's territory in 1276, and by 1277 forced Llywelyn to accept terms, reducing his territory to a rump of Gwynedd. A rebellion in 1282 collapsed following the death of Llywelyn. In 1284 Wales was incorporated into England under the Statute of Rhuddlan. Edward's son and heir, Edward of Caernarfon, was created Prince of Wales by the Lincoln Parliament of 1301.

This list covers South Welsh armies from 1100 until 1197 and North Welsh armies from 1100 until 1283.

TROOP NOTES

In South Welsh forces of this period archers predominated, while in the North spearmen were the more numerous type. Little, if any, protective armour was worn, and although some spearmen carried shields, many depictions show them without. Although raids and ambushes were preferred, Welsh armies did engage in pitched battles from time to time.

North Welsh Spearman

NORTH WELSH STARTER ARMY 1225 AD		
Commander-in-Chief	1	Field Commander
Sub-commanders	2	2 x Troop Commander
Cavalry	1 BG	4 bases of cavalry: Superior, Armoured, Undrilled Cavalry – Lancers, Swordsmen
Cavalry	1 BG	4 bases of cavalry: Superior, Protected, Undrilled Cavalry – Lancers, Swordsmen
Cavalry	1 BG	4 bases of cavalry: Average, Unprotected, Undrilled Light Horse – Javelins, Light Spear
Spearmen	4 BGs	Each comprising 10 bases of spearmen: Average, Unprotected, Undrilled Medium Foot – Offensive Spearmen
Archers	2 BGs	Each comprising 8 bases of archers: Average, Unprotected, Undrilled Light Foot – Longbow
Camp	1	Unfortified camp
Total	9 BGs	Camp, 12 mounted bases, 56 foot bases, 3 commanders

BUILDING A CUSTOMISED LIST USING OUR ARMY POINTS

Choose an army based on the maxima and minima in the list below. The following special instructions apply to this army:

- Commanders should be depicted as cavalry or spearmen.
- Cavalry can always dismount as Superior, Armoured or Protected (as mounted type), Undrilled Heavy Foot – Impact Foot, Swordsmen.

- The army must be North Welsh or South Welsh.
- North Welsh armies can have North Welsh and/or South Welsh allies. Troops included in these allied contingents are deducted from the North Welsh minima and maxima in the main list, except that a North Welsh army with South Welsh allies can have up to 32 bases of archers
- South Welsh armies can have South Welsh allies. Troops included in this allied contingent are deducted from the South Welsh minima and maxima in the main list.

LATER WELSH

Territory Types: Mountains, Hilly, Woodlands

C-in-C	Inspired Commander/Field Commander/Troop Commander				80/50/35	1	
Sub-commanders	Field Commander				50	0–2	
	Troop Commander				35	0–3	

Troop name	Troop Type				Capabilities		Points per base	Bases per BG	Total bases	
	Type	Armour	Quality	Training	Shooting	Close Combat				
Core Troops										
Cavalry	Cavalry	Armoured	Superior	Undrilled	–	Light Spear, Swordsmen	16	4	0–4	4–12
	Cavalry	Armoured	Superior	Undrilled	–	Lancers, Swordsman	16	4		
	Cavalry	Protected	Superior	Undrilled	–	Light Spear, Swordsmen	12	4–6	0–12	
	Cavalry	Protected	Superior	Undrilled	–	Lancers, Swordsman	12	4–6		
	Light Horse	Unprotected	Average	Undrilled	Javelins	Light Spear	7	4–6	0–8	
	Light Horse	Unprotected	Average	Undrilled	–	Lancers, Swordsman	8	4–6		
Archers	Medium Foot	Unprotected	Average	Undrilled	Longbow	–	6	6–8	0–136	North Welsh 0–24, South Welsh 32–142
	Light Foot	Unprotected	Average	Undrilled	Longbow	–	6	6–8	0–16	
Spearmen	Medium Foot	Unprotected	Average	Undrilled	–	Offensive Spearmen	6	6–10	0–136	North Welsh 32–142, South Welsh 0–24
	Light Foot	Unprotected	Average	Undrilled	Javelins	Light spear	4	6–8	0–16	
Allies										

English marcher allies (Only from 1150) – Early Plantaganet English

Irish mercenary allies (Only before 1150) – Norse Irish – See Field of Glory Companion 8: *Wolves from the Sea: The Dark Ages*

North Welsh allies (Only North Welsh) – Later Welsh

South Welsh allies – Later Welsh

LATER WELSH ALLIES

Troop name	Troop Type				Capabilities		Points per base	Bases per BG	Total bases	
	Type	Armour	Quality	Training	Shooting	Close Combat				
Cavalry	Cavalry	Protected	Superior	Undrilled	–	Light Spear, Swordsmen	12	4	0–4	0–4
	Cavalry	Protected	Superior	Undrilled	–	Lancers, Swordsman	12	4		
	Light Horse	Unprotected	Average	Undrilled	Javelins	Light Spear	7	4	0–4	
	Light Horse	Unprotected	Average	Undrilled	–	Lancers, Swordsman	8	4		
Archers	Medium Foot	Unprotected	Average	Undrilled	Longbow	–	6	6–8	0–32	North Welsh 0–8, South Welsh 8–32
	Light Foot	Unprotected	Average	Undrilled	Longbow	–	6	4–6	0–6	
Spearmen	Medium Foot	Unprotected	Average	Undrilled	–	Offensive Spearmen	6	6–10	0–32	North Welsh 8–32, South Welsh 0–8
	Light Foot	Unprotected	Average	Undrilled	Javelins	Light spear	4	4–6	0–6	

EARLY LITHUANIAN OR SAMOGITIAN

The Lithuanians and Samogitians comprised a number of related Baltic tribes in the area of modern Lithuania. The first historical mention of Lithuania is in monastic annals dated 1009 AD. In the 11th century the Lithuanian tribes paid tribute to Kievan Rus, but by the 12th century their raids on neighbouring territories had become troublesome.

The threat posed by the Teutonic Knights to the west and the Livonian Brothers of the Sword to the north resulted in the unification of the Lithuanian tribes by Mindaugas, who inflicted a severe defeat on the Sword Brethren at the Battle of Šiauliai (Saule) in 1236. Following this disaster the depleted Sword Brethren were absorbed into the Teutonic Order, with whom Mindaugas signed a treaty in 1250. By the terms of this treaty he transferred parts of Samogitia to the Order. He was baptized in 1251 and crowned as the first and only King of Lithuania in 1253.

Following the defeat of the Teutonic Order by the Samogitians at the Battle of Durbe in 1260, however, Mindaugas renounced the treaty. It is uncertain whether he also renounced Christianity, but after his assassination by his nephew Treniota in 1263, Lithuania certainly reverted to paganism and ceased to be recognised as a Kingdom.

For the rest of the century Lithuania was in conflict with the Teutonic Order, the Polish Duchy of Masovia and the local Russian principalities. In addition, Lithuania suffered Mongol (Tatar) raids in 1241, 1259 and 1275.

By the end of the reign of Grand Duke Vytenis (1295–1316), however, Lithuania had expanded to include Lithuania proper, Samogitia (modern western Lithuania), Red Russia (in western Ukraine) and Polatsk and Minsk (in Belarus). In the 14th century, territorial gains continued. In 1386 Lithuania was joined in dynastic union with Poland.

This list covers the Lithuanians and related Samogitians from 1100 until 1300.

TROOP NOTES

Lithuanian cavalry were equipped with a shortish light "lance" which could be thrust or thrown. They also carried a 1 metre (3 foot) self bow, which in this period was only used when dismounted. They were fond of skirmishing and ambushes, often dismounting to fight in woodlands. Boyars fought surrounded by their less well-equipped followers. We assume that only the best equipped contingents would have enough armoured men to justify classification as Armoured.

Lithuanian Commander

EARLY LITHUANIAN STARTER ARMY 1250 AD

Commander-in-Chief	1	Troop Commander
Sub-commanders	2	2 x Troop Commander
Best cavalry	3 BGs	Each comprising 4 bases of best cavalry: Superior, Armoured, Undrilled Cavalry – Light Spear, Swordsmen
Other cavalry	5 BGs	Each comprising 4 bases of other cavalry: Average, Unprotected, Undrilled Light Horse – Javelins, Light Spear, Swordsmen
Spearmen	2 BGs	Each comprising 6 bases of spearmen: Average, Protected, Undrilled Medium Foot – Light Spear
Archers	2 BGs	Each comprising 6 bases of archers: Average, Unprotected, Undrilled Light Foot – Bow
Camp	1	Unfortified camp
Total	12 BGs	Camp, 32 mounted bases, 24 foot bases, 3 commanders

BUILDING A CUSTOMISED LIST USING OUR ARMY POINTS

Choose an army based on the maxima and minima in the list below. The following special instructions apply to this army:

- Commanders should be depicted as armoured Lithuanian cavalry.

- Best cavalry can always dismount as Superior, Undrilled Medium Foot – Bow, Swordsmen. (Armour class the same as when mounted).

- Other cavalry can always dismount as Light Foot or Medium Foot (free choice), Undrilled, Bow. (Armour class the same as when mounted).

Lithuanian Spearmen

EARLY LITHUANIAN OR SAMOGITIAN

Territory Types: Agricultural, Woodlands, Steppes

C-in-C		Inspired Commander/Field Commander/Troop Commander					80/50/35		1	
Sub-commanders		Field Commander					50		0–2	
		Troop Commander					35		0–3	
Troop name		Troop Type				Capabilities		Points per base	Bases per BG	Total bases
		Type	Armour	Quality	Training	Shooting	Close Combat			
Core Troops										
Best cavalry	Any date	Cavalry	Protected	Superior	Undrilled	–	Light Spear, Swordsmen	12	4–6	0–12	24–116
	Only from 1200	Cavalry	Armoured	Superior	Undrilled	–	Light Spear, Swordsmen	16	4–6		
Other cavalry	Any date	Light Horse	Unprotected	Average	Undrilled	Javelins	Light Spear, Swordsmen	9	4–6	16–116	
		Cavalry	Unprotected	Average	Undrilled	–	Light Spear, Swordsmen	8	4–6		
			Protected					9			
Spearmen		Medium Foot	Protected	Average	Undrilled	–	Light Spear	5	6–8	0–12	
Archers		Light Foot	Unprotected	Average	Undrilled	Bow	–	5	6–8	0–12	
		Medium foot	Unprotected	Average	Undrilled	Bow	–	5	6–8		
Optional Troops										
Replace other cavalry with foot archers		Light Foot	Unprotected	Average	Undrilled	Bow	–	5	6–8	Before 1200 Any, From 1200 Up to half
		Medium Foot	Unprotected	Average	Undrilled	Bow	–	5	6–8	
Field fortifications		Field Fortifications						3		0–12
Fortified camp								24		0–1
Allies										
Teutonic Knights allies (Only from 1250 to 1253) – Early Teutonic Knights										

WENDISH, PRUSSIAN OR ESTONIAN

This list covers the various pagan Slavic or Baltic tribes in the Baltic region that were conquered by a series of Crusades in the 12th and 13th centuries AD. Lithuania is covered by its own list.

Wendland was conquered by German and Danish crusaders by 1185. Prussia was conquered by the Teutonic Knights by 1283. Estonia was conquered by the Danes and the Livonian Sword Brethren by 1227.

The list covers Wendish armies from 1100 to 1185, Pomeranian allied contingents thereafter until the late 13th century, Prussian armies from 1200 to 1283 and Estonian armies from 1200 to 1227.

TROOP NOTES

The mounted upper class warriors were more likely to fight dismounted further to the east – the Estonians rode to battle but customarily fought on foot.

Foot were mainly armed with thrusting spears, throwing spears, throwing axes, swords and hand axes. They lacked armour but mostly carried smallish kite shields. The preferred tactic was to throw spears and then charge – although mounted knights were usually received at the halt. The sources indicate that Prussian lower class warriors often lacked the enthusiasm of their betters. We assume that the same may have been true of the other Baltic tribes.

WENDISH STARTER ARMY 1180 AD		
Commander-in-Chief	1	Field Commander
Sub-commanders	2	2 x Troop Commander
Upper class warriors	1 BG	4 bases of upper class warriors: Superior, Armoured, Undrilled Cavalry – Light Spear, Swordsmen
Upper class warriors	2 BGs	Each comprising 4 bases of upper class warriors: Superior, Protected, Undrilled Cavalry – Light Spear, Swordsmen
Danish or Saxon mercenaries	1 BG	4 bases of Danish or Saxon mercenaries: Superior, Heavily Armoured, Undrilled Knights – Lancers, Swordsmen
Lower class warriors	3 BGs	Each comprising 8 bases of lower class warriors: Average, Protected, Undrilled Medium Foot – Impact Foot, Swordsmen
Archers	2 BGs	Each comprising 6 bases of archers: Average, Unprotected, Undrilled Light Foot – Bow
Camp	1	Unfortified camp
Total	9 BGs	Camp, 16 mounted bases, 36 foot bases, 3 commanders

BUILDING A CUSTOMISED LIST USING OUR ARMY POINTS

Choose an army based on the maxima and minima in the list below. The following special instructions apply to this army:

Lower Class Warrior

- Commanders should be depicted as mounted warriors.
- Prussian upper class warriors can always dismount as Superior, Protected, Undrilled Medium Foot – Impact Foot, Swordsmen.

WENDISH, PRUSSIAN OR ESTONIAN

Territory Types: Agricultural, Woodlands

C-in-C	Inspired Commander/Field Commander/Troop Commander			80/50/35	1	
Sub-commanders	Field Commander			50	0–2	
	Troop Commander			35	0–3	

Troop name		Troop Type				Capabilities		Points per base	Bases per BG	Total bases	
		Type	Armour	Quality	Training	Shooting	Close Combat				
Core Troops											
Upper class warriors	Only Wends	Cavalry	Armoured	Superior	Undrilled	–	Light Spear, Swordsmen	16	4	0–4	4–16
	Only Wends or Prussians	Cavalry	Protected	Superior	Undrilled	–	Light Spear, Swordsmen	12	4–6	0–16	
	Only Estonians	Medium Foot	Protected	Superior	Undrilled	–	Impact Foot, Swordsmen	9	6–8	6–16	
Lower class warriors		Medium Foot	Protected	Average	Undrilled	–	Impact Foot, Swordsmen	7	8–12	24–128	
				Poor				5			
Archers		Medium Foot	Protected	Average	Undrilled	Bow	–	6	6–8	6–24	
				Poor				4			
		Light Foot	Unprotected	Average	Undrilled	Bow	–	5	6–8		
				Poor				3			
Optional Troops											
Danish or Saxon mercenaries	Only Wends at any date	Knights	Armoured	Superior	Undrilled	–	Lancers, Swordsmen	20	4	0–4	
				Average				16			
	Only Wends from 1150	Knights	Heavily Armoured	Superior	Undrilled	–	Lancers, Swordsmen	23	4		
				Average				18			
Crossbowmen	Only Estonians	Medium Foot	Protected	Average	Undrilled	Crossbow	–	6	4–6	0–6	
		Light Foot	Unprotected	Average	Undrilled	Bow	–	5	4–6		
Barricades		Field Fortifications	–	–	–	–	–	3	–	0–12	
Allies											

Pomeranian (Wendish) allies (Only Prussians) – Wendish, Prussian or Estonian

Russian allies (Only Estonians) – Early Russian

WENDISH, PRUSSIAN OR ESTONIAN ALLIES

Allied commander	Field Commander/Troop Commander							40/25	1		
Troop name		Troop Type				Capabilities		Points per base	Bases per BG	Total bases	
		Type	Armour	Quality	Training	Shooting	Close Combat				
Upper class warriors	Only Wends	Cavalry	Armoured	Superior	Undrilled	–	Light Spear, Swordsmen	16	4	0–4	4–6
	Only Wends or Prussians	Cavalry	Protected	Superior	Undrilled	–	Light Spear, Swordsmen	12	4–6	0–6	
	Only Estonians	Medium Foot	Protected	Superior	Undrilled	–	Impact Foot, Swordsmen	9	4–6	4–6	
Lower class warriors		Medium Foot	Protected	Average	Undrilled	–	Impact Foot, Swordsmen	7	8–12	8–24	
				Poor				5			
Archers		Medium Foot	Protected	Average	Undrilled	Bow	–	6	6–8	0–8	
				Poor				4			
		Light Foot	Unprotected	Average	Undrilled	Bow	–	5	6–8		
				Poor				3			

EARLY MEDIEVAL FRISIA AND OTHER FREE CANTONS

Frisia was the largest of the 'autonomous peasant republics' also known as the Free Cantons. Smaller Free Cantons included Dithmarchen and Stedinger, and may or may not have included North Frisia. While formally belonging to this or that powerful noble or city they were effectively independent.

This list covers Free Canton armies from the earliest time they are mentioned in 1106 (1144 for Dithmarchen) until 1340. Frisia and Dithmarchen continued to maintain their independence until the late 15th century, although the Stedinger Republic fell to a crusading alliance led by the Duke of Brabant in 1234.

Friesland especially was by no means a unified area. Internal strife was common, but rarely took the form of field battles, lightning raids being much more common. Whenever outside powers tried to take advantage, however, they usually found the Free Cantoners united, with all internal squabbles suspended.

All attempts to bring them to heel failed, often at great cost to the would-be conquerors. In large part this was due to the inaccessible terrain. It also helped that most of the nominal overlords were not that interested in subjugating these people, realizing the cost of doing so and the comparably low value of what they stood to gain.

Now and then parts of the Free Cantons, especially Frisia with its prosperous cities, were formally subjugated. They usually soon revolted, however, renouncing all obligations to their so called overlords. At times they invited outside powers to protect them, but never for long.

The Stedingers struggled against the Archbishops of Bremen, who tried to force them to submit by excommunicating them. After this failed, a crusade was called against them. They defeated the first army send against them in 1233 but were defeated by a large alliance of 'crusaders', mainly made up by troops of the Duke of Brabant, the Count of Oldenburg and the Arch-Bishop of Bremen, in 1234.

Like Stedingen, Dithmarchen formally belonged to the Archbishop of Bremen, but the one time they were more or less completely conquered was by the Danes in 1219, who then made the error of incorporating Dithmarchen troops into their army. The very next battle the Dithmarchen contingents switched sides and attacked the rear of the Danes while they were frontally engaged with their German opponents. The resulting Danish defeat effectively freed Dithmarchen again from Danish rule.

TROOP NOTES

Due to the terrain these armies fought in and their defensive strategies their knights seem to have fought mainly dismounted.

The "fortifications" used were sometimes palisades or earth walls, but in most cases consisted of drainage channels.

The pole spear used by the Free Cantoners was held in both hands, precluding the use of a shield. It had a disk on the butt end (up to 20 cm in diameter) to prevent it sinking into the mud when it was used as a 'vaulting pole' to

Dismounted Free Canton Knight

quickly and safely jump over drainage channels, small bogs or other treacherous terrain features. This allowed the users unmatched mobility in marshy terrain. There is also mention of long

swords, axes and similar weapons. We subsume these into the spearmen, however, as their numbers were probably not great, nor does it seem that they were used in separate units.

EARLY MEDIEVAL FRISIAN STARTER ARMY 1275 AD		
Commander-in-Chief	1	Field Commander
Sub-commanders	2	2 x Troop Commander
Knights	1 BG	4 bases of knights: Superior, Heavily Armoured, Undrilled Knights – Lancers, Swordsmen
Pole spearmen	5 BGs	Each comprising 8 bases of pole spearmen: Average, Protected, Undrilled Medium Foot – Offensive Spearmen
Skirmishing javelinmen	1 BG	6 bases of skirmishing javelinmen: Average, Unprotected, Undrilled Light Foot – Javelins, Light Spear
Crossbowmen	1 BG	6 bases of crossbowmen: Average, Unprotected, Undrilled Light Foot – Crossbow
Archers	1 BG	6 bases of archers: Average, Unprotected, Undrilled Light Foot – Bow
Field fortifications	8	8 bases frontage of drainage channels, palisades or earth walls
Camp	1	Unfortified camp
Total	9 BGs	Camp, 4 mounted bases, 58 foot bases, 3 commanders, 8 bases frontage of field fortifications

BUILDING A CUSTOMISED LIST USING OUR ARMY POINTS

Choose an army based on the maxima and minima in the list below. The following special instructions apply to this army:

- Commanders should be depicted as pole spearmen or knights.
- Knights can always dismount as Superior, Heavily Armoured, Undrilled Heavy Foot – Heavy Weapon.
- Stedinger cannot use any non-allied Knights.

- Free Canton allied commanders' contingents must conform to the Early Medieval Frisian or other Free Canton allies list below, but the troops in the contingent are deducted from the minima and maxima in the main list.
- Only one ally contingent can be used.

Pole Spearman

EARLY MEDIEVAL FRISIA AND OTHER FREE CANTONS

Territory Types: Agricultural, Woodlands

C-in-C	Inspired Commander/Field Commander/Troop Commander					80/50/35	1	
Sub-commanders	Field Commander					50	0–2	
	Troop Commander					35	0–3	
Free Canton allied commanders	Field Commander/Troop Commander					40/25	0–2	

Troop name		Troop Type				Capabilities		Points per base	Bases per BG	Total bases
		Type	Armour	Quality	Training	Shooting	Impact			
Core Troops										
Free Canton knights	Only from 1200	Knights	Heavily Armoured	Superior	Undrilled	–	Lancers Swordsmen	23	4	0–4
		Heavy Foot	Heavily Armoured	Superior	Undrilled	–	Heavy Weapon	14	4	
Pole spearmen		Medium Foot	Protected	Average	Undrilled	–	Offensive Spearmen	7	6–10	24–130
			Unprotected					6		
Crossbowmen		Medium Foot	Protected	Average	Undrilled	Crossbow	–	6	6–8	0–12 / 6–12
			Unprotected					5		
		Light Foot	Unprotected	Average	Undrilled	Crossbow	–	5	6–8	0–8
Archers		Medium Foot	Protected	Average	Undrilled	Bow	–	6	6–8	0–8
			Unprotected					5		
		Light Foot	Unprotected	Average	Undrilled	Bow	–	5	6–8	
Skirmishing javelinmen		Light Foot	Unprotected	Average	Undrilled	Javelins	Light Spear	4	6–8	6–24
Drainage ditches or other field fortifications		Field Fortifications						3		8–48
Optional Troops										
Fortified camp								24		0–1
Allies										
Danish allies – Post–Viking Scandinavian (only Frisia or Dithmarchen)										
German allies – German Ecclesiastical (only Stedinger), German City (only Dithmarchen) or German Feudal allies (only Frisia or Dithmarchen)										

EARLY MEDIEVAL FRISIAN OR OTHER FREE CANTON ALLIES

Allied commander	Field Commander/Troop Commander					40/25	1	
Troop name	Troop Type				Capabilities		Points per base	Bases per BG	Total bases

Troop name	Type	Armour	Quality	Training	Shooting	Impact	Points per base	Bases per BG	Total bases
Pole spearmen	Medium Foot	Protected	Average	Undrilled	–	Offensive Spearmen	7	6–10	8–24
		Unprotected					6		
Crossbowmen	Medium Foot	Protected	Average	Undrilled	Crossbow	–	6	4	0–4
		Unprotected					5		
	Light Foot	Unprotected	Average	Undrilled	Crossbow	–	5	4	
Archers	Medium Foot	Protected	Average	Undrilled	Bow	–	6	4	
		Unprotected					5		
	Light Foot	Unprotected					5		
Skirmishing javelinmen	Light Foot	Unprotected	Average	Undrilled	Javelins	Light Spear	4	6–8	0–8

POST-VIKING SCANDINAVIAN

This list covers Scandinavian armies from 1150 until 1300.

At the start of this period, after a period of civil war, Denmark was united under the rule of Valdemar the Great (1131–1182). Valdemar built Denmark into a major power in the Baltic region. He and his successors launched several "crusades" against the pagan tribes of the Baltic, adding parts of Wendland and northern Estonia to the Danish kingdom. By the late 13th century, however, the power of the Danish monarchy had declined, with the Counts of Holstein owning much of the country.

Norway suffered a series of civil wars between 1130 and 1240, when King Håkon Håkonsson defeated his last royal rival. Håkon brought Iceland and Greenland under Norwegian rule. Orkney, the Western Isles of Scotland and the Isle of Man were already at least theoretically subject to Norwegian rule, but Haakon's attempt to enforce these rights failed following the Battle of Largs in 1263 and he died on his way back to Norway. By the terms of the Treaty of Perth (1266), his son and successor Magnus VI the Law-Mender gave up his claim to the Western Isles and Man but retained control of Orkney.

From 1130 the throne of Sweden alternated for several generations between the rival houses of Sverker in Östergötland and Eric in Uppland, until in the 1220s the Eric dynasty got the upper hand, and the Sverker dynasty became extinct in the male line. In 1250 Valdemar Birgersson ascended the throne, having inherited both Eric and Sverker dynastic claims through his mother and grandmother. He was the first king of the House of Bjälbo, which ruled Sweden until the late 14th century. At some time circa 1249 Sweden conquered parts of Finland, although details of the conquest are obscure, and further areas were annexed in 1293.

TROOP NOTES

The mainstay of Scandinavian armies in this period was still the infantry shieldwall (skjaldborg), comprising men armed with various combinations of sword, axe, throwing spears and thrusting spears. This formation is best represented under the rules as Offensive Spearmen. Archers would form up in the rear ranks. They can be represented separately as supporting light foot, or assumed to be included in the overall effect of the shieldwall.

Hirdmen were paid household troops, and continued to make much use of the traditional two-handed axe.

Mounted knights were increasingly important, however, particularly in Denmark, although always heavily outnumbered by the infantry. The development of Scandinavian knightly armour lagged slightly behind that of the rest of Europe, but not by much.

Hirdman

Swedish forces at the Battle of Hova, 1275, by Angus McBride. Taken from Men-at-Arms 396:
Medieval Scandinavian Armies (1): 1100–1300

DANISH STARTER ARMY 1250 AD		
Commander-in-Chief	1	Field Commander
Sub-commanders	2	2 x Troop Commander
Knights	2 BGs	Each comprising 4 bases of knights: Superior, Heavily Armoured, Undrilled Knights – Lancers, Swordsmen
Leidang	4 BGs	Each comprising 8 bases of Leidang: Average, Protected, Undrilled Heavy Foot – Offensive Spearmen
Crossbowmen	1 BG	6 bases of crossbowmen: Average, Protected, Undrilled Medium Foot – Crossbow
Archers	1 BG	6 bases of archers: Average, Unprotected, Undrilled Light Foot – Bow
Camp	1	Unfortified camp
Total	8 BGs	Camp, 8 mounted bases, 44 foot bases, 3 commanders

BUILDING A CUSTOMISED LIST USING OUR ARMY POINTS

Choose an army based on the maxima and minima in the list below. The following special instructions apply to this army:

• Commanders should be depicted as hirdmen or knights.

• Knights can always dismount as Superior, Armoured or Heavily Armoured (as mounted type), Undrilled, Heavy Foot – Heavy Weapon.

Dismounted Knight

POST-VIKING SCANDINAVIAN									
Territory Types: Agricultural, Woodland									
C-in-C		Inspired Commander/Field Commander/Troop Commander					80/50/35	1	
Sub-commanders		Field Commander					50	0–2	
		Troop Commander					35	0–3	
Troop name		Troop Type				Capabilities		Points per base	Bases per BG	Total bases
		Type	Armour	Quality	Training	Shooting	Impact			
Core Troops										
Hirdmen or knights	Norway or Sweden at any date, Denmark only before 1200	Heavy Foot	Armoured	Superior	Undrilled	–	Heavy Weapon	12	2/3 or all	6–9	0–18
		Light Foot	Unprotected	Superior	Undrilled	Bow	–	6	1/3 or 0		
	Only before 1200	Knights	Armoured	Superior	Undrilled	–	Lancers, Swordsmen	20	4–6	4–18
				Average				16		
	Any date	Knights	Heavily Armoured	Superior	Undrilled	–	Lancers, Swordsmen	23	4–6	0–12
				Average				18		
Leidang		Heavy Foot	Protected	Average	Undrilled	–	Offensive Spearmen	7	2/3 or all	8–9	20–108
		Light Foot	Unprotected	Average	Undrilled	Bow	–	5	1/3 or 0		
Optional Troops										
Mounted crossbowmen	Only Denmark from 1200	Cavalry	Armoured	Average	Drilled	Crossbow	Swordsmen	14	4	0–4
					Undrilled			13		
Separately deployed archers		Light Foot	Unprotected	Average	Undrilled	Bow	–	5	6–8	0–8
Crossbowmen		Medium Foot	Protected	Average	Undrilled	Crossbow	–	6	6–8	0–12
Fortified camp								24		0–1
Allies										
German Ecclesiastical allies (Only Danish)										
Wendish allies (Only Danish from 1219) – Wendish, Prussian or Estonian										

POST-VIKING SCANDINAVIAN ALLIES

Allied commander		Field Commander/Troop Commander					40/25	1	
Troop name		Troop Type				Capabilities		Points per base	Bases per BG	Total bases
		Type	Armour	Quality	Training	Shooting	Impact			
Hirdmen or knights	Norway or Sweden at any date, Denmark only before 1200	Heavy Foot	Armoured	Superior	Undrilled	–	Heavy Weapon	12	2/3 or all	4–6	0–6
		Light Foot	Unprotected	Superior	Undrilled	Bow	–	6	1/3 or 0	
	Only before 1200	Knights	Armoured	Superior	Undrilled	–	Lancers, Swordsmen	20	4	4–6
				Average				16		0–4
	Any date	Knights	Heavily Armoured	Superior	Undrilled	–	Lancers, Swordsmen	23	4	
				Average				18		
Leidang		Heavy Foot	Protected	Average	Undrilled	–	Offensive Spearmen	7	2/3 or all	8–9	6–27
		Light Foot	Unprotected	Average	Undrilled	Bow	–	5	1/3 or 0	
Crossbowmen		Medium Foot	Protected	Average	Undrilled	Crssbow	–	6	4	0–4

The Danish Invasion of the Island of Rügen, 1168–69, by Angus McBride. Taken from Men-at-Arms 436: The Scandinavian Baltic Crusades 1100–1500

EARLY PLANTAGENET ENGLISH

On the death of King Stephen in 1154 AD, Henry II ascended the throne as previously agreed. Having inherited Anjou and Maine from his father Geoffrey Plantaganet, and Normandy as a possession of the English Crown, he had also acquired Aquitaine, Gascony and Poitou through his marriage to Eleanor of Aquitaine in 1152. He thus already possessed control of most of western France, and rounded this off by forcing Conan, Duke of Brittany to accept vassal status and subsequently making his son Geoffrey Duke of Brittany by marrying him to Conan's heiress. He also sponsored the Anglo-Norman invasion of Ireland under the leadership of the Earl of Pembroke, Richard de Clare. Henry travelled to Ireland in 1171 and named his youngest son, John, "Lord of Ireland".

Henry's later years were marred by rebellion by his sons and by internecine strife between them. Two of them, Henry and Geoffrey, died before their father, leaving Richard I as heir to the throne when Henry died, a broken man, in 1189.

Soon after ascending the throne, Richard began to make arrangements to set forth on the Third Crusade – agreeing with King Philip II of France that both of them should go, thus reducing the risk of either taking advantage of the other's absence to attack his territories.

English Knight

The Crusade was a qualified success (see Field of Glory Companion 4: *Swords and Scimitars*) but Richard was absent from 1190 to 1194, having been detained by Leopold V of Austria since 1192. On his return he was reconciled to his youngest brother, John, who had come close to seizing the throne. War with France followed. Richard died in 1199 after being wounded by a crossbow bolt at the siege of a minor castle.

He was succeeded by his brother John. The succession was not universally accepted, however, with many nobles in the French territories supporting his nephew Arthur of Brittany, son of Geoffrey, as the rightful heir. King Philip supported Arthur. He subsequently declared all John's French possessions except Gascony forfeit, and granted all except Normandy to Arthur. Arthur, however, was captured in 1203 and murdered by John's agents. This caused Brittany and Normandy to rebel against John. In 1214 an alliance between John and the Holy Roman Emperor Otto IV was shattered when the latter was defeated by the French at the Battle of Bouvines. John was forced to accept a humiliating peace, retaining only Gascony of all his inherited French possessions, and was also forced to sign Magna Carta by his rebellious English barons. In 1216 the barons offered the English throne to Prince Louis of France, who arrived with an army and was proclaimed King of England at London, though not crowned. Retreating from the French invasion, John fell ill and died. His son, the 9-year old Henry III, was hastily crowned at Gloucester. Gradually the barons went over to his side until Louis was forced to sign the Treaty of Lambeth in 1217, in which he acknowledged that he had never been the legitimate King of England.

The Battle of Lewes, 14 May 1264, by Graham Turner. Taken from *Warrior* 48: English Medieval Knight 1200–1300

Henry III reigned until his death in 1272. Though long, his reign was not successful and was marred by civil war against the barons. He was succeeded by his son Edward I, a far more forceful and militarily successful character.

This list covers the armies of the Angevin "Empire" in England and France from 1154 to 1216, and English armies from 1216 to 1272.

TROOP NOTES

During the "Empire" period troops could equally be English or French in origin. In Henry III's reign most would be English.

Contemporary illustrations suggest that infantry were armed with heavy cutting weapons and swords as often as spears. However it is likely that they fought in mixed bodies as described in the Catalan list. We treat such mixed bodies as Spearmen.

Welsh archerii were mounted Welsh archers. We do not accept the notion that they fought mounted.

Irish troops were used in quite large numbers in Wales and Scotland in the 13th century, usually serving under their own kings.

EARLY PLANTAGENET ENGLISH STARTER ARMY 1200 AD		
Commander-in-Chief	1	Field Commander
Sub-commanders	2	2 x Troop Commander
Feudal knights	2 BGs	Each comprising 4 bases of feudal knights: Superior, Heavily Armoured, Undrilled Knights – Lancers, Swordsmen
Mounted crossbowmen	1 BG	4 bases of mounted crossbowmen: Average, Armoured, Undrilled Cavalry – Crossbow, Swordsmen
Welsh equites	1 BG	4 bases of Welsh equites: Average, Unprotected, Undrilled Light Horse – Javelins, Light Spear
Foot sergeants and English freemen	2 BGs	Each comprising 8 bases of foot sergeants and English freemen: Average, Protected, Undrilled Heavy Foot – Defensive Spearmen
Crossbowmen	1 BG	8 bases of crossbowmen: Average, Protected, Undrilled Medium Foot – Crossbow
Welsh infantry	1 BG	8 bases of Welsh Infantry: Average, Unprotected, Undrilled Medium Foot – Offensive Spearmen
Welsh archerii	1 BG	4 bases of Welsh archerii: Average, Unprotected, Undrilled Medium Foot – Longbow
Camp	1	Unfortified camp
Total	9 BGs	Camp, 16 mounted bases, 36 foot bases, 3 commanders

BUILDING A CUSTOMISED LIST USING OUR ARMY POINTS

Choose an army based on the maxima and minima in the list below. The following special instructions apply to this army:

- Commanders should be depicted as knights.

- Welsh *equites* can always dismount as Average, Unprotected, Undrilled Medium Foot – Offensive Spearmen.
- No more than one allied contingent can be used.

*Feudal
Crossbowman*

EARLY PLANTAGENET ENGLISH

Territory Types: Agricultural, Woodlands

C-in-C		Inspired Commander/Field Commander/Troop Commander					80/50/35		1	
Sub-commanders		Field Commander					50		0–2	
		Troop Commander					35		0–3	
Troop name		Troop Type				Capabilities		Points per base	Bases per BG	Total bases
		Type	Armour	Quality	Training	Shooting	Close Combat			
Core Troops										
Knights and sergeants		Knights	Heavily Armoured	Superior	Undrilled	–	Lancers, Swordsmen	23	4–6	6–32
Foot sergeants and English freemen		Heavy Foot	Protected	Average	Undrilled	–	Defensive Spearmen	6	6–8	0–24
				Poor				4		
Mercenary spearmen		Heavy Foot	Armoured	Average	Drilled	–	Defensive Spearmen	9	6–8	0–8
			Protected					7		
Town militia		Heavy Foot	Protected	Poor	Drilled	–	Defensive Spearmen	5	6–8	0–24
Optional Troops										
Separately deployed sergeants		Cavalry	Armoured	Average	Undrilled	–	Lancers, Swordsmen	12	4–6	0–6
Mounted crossbowmen		Cavalry	Armoured	Average	Undrilled	Crossbow	Swordsmen	13	4	0–4
Welsh equites		Light Horse	Unprotected	Average	Undrilled	Javelins	Light Spear	7	4	0–4
		Cavalry	Protected	Average	Undrilled	–	Light Spear, Swordsmen	9	4	
Mercenary knights and sergeants		Knights	Heavily Armoured	Superior	Undrilled	–	Lancers, Swordsmen	23	4–6	0–6
Feudal crossbowmen		Medium Foot	Protected	Average	Undrilled	Crossbow	–	6	6–8	0–8
Mercenary crossbowmen		Medium Foot	Protected	Average	Drilled	Crossbow	–	7	6–8	
Foot archers		Light Foot	Unprotected	Average	Undrilled	Bow	–	5	6–8	0–8
		Medium Foot	Unprotected	Average	Undrilled	Bow	–	5	6–8	
Welsh archerii		Medium Foot	Unprotected	Average	Undrilled	Longbow	–	6	4	0–4
Welsh infantry		Medium Foot	Unprotected	Average	Undrilled	–	Offensive Spearmen	6	6–8	0–16
Galwegian foot	Only in Britain	Medium Foot	Protected	Average	Undrilled	–	Impact Foot, Swordsmen	7	6–8	0–8
			Unprotected					6		
Irish foot	Only in Britain from 1242	Medium Foot	Unprotected	Average	Undrilled	–	Heavy Weapon	6	4–6	0–6
		Medium Foot	Unprotected	Average	Undrilled	–	Light Spear, Swordsmen	5	4–6	
		Light Foot	Unprotected	Average	Undrilled	Javelins	Light Spear	4	4–6	
Allies										

Mercenary spearmen and Town militia share a combined total of 12–48.

Allies
Only in Britain
Dublin Viking Allies (Only before 1169) – Viking – See Field of Glory Companion 8: *Wolves from the Sea: The Dark Ages*
Irish allies (Only from 1242) – Early Medieval Irish
North or South Welsh allies – Later Welsh
Scots Allies – Feudal Scots
Only in France
French Allies – Feudal French
Navarrese allies (Only from 1194 to 1196) – Feudal Navarrese and Aragonese

LATER SICILIAN

This list covers the armies of the Kingdom of Sicily from the death of Roger II in 1154 until the Kingdom was split by the War of the Sicilian Vespers in 1282. Thereafter it covers the armies of the Angevin Kingdom of Naples until 1320 and those of the Kingdom of Sicily until the union with Naples in 1442.

The last Norman kings were kept busy mostly by their own nobility who (sometimes supported by the Byzantines) tended to be rather rebellious. Nevertheless, some of them managed to put their considerable military power to use on occasion, such as William II's campaign in Greece.

After William died without male heirs, the German King Heinrich VI claimed the throne in the right of his wife Constance, posthumous daughter of Roger II of Sicily. He failed to enforce his claim until 1194, however, allowing Tancred, an illegitimate grandson of Roger II, to become the last reigning Norman King of Sicily.

Heinrich VI was followed by his son Friedrich II who managed to keep the still rebellious Norman nobility under control and put down and later win the loyalty of the Saracens. From 1235 Friedrich largely undertook his military endeavours with an army based on his Sicilian Kingdom rather than his German holdings.

After his death his son Konrad IV, having been driven from Germany, assumed the Sicilian throne. Unlike his father he proved unable to stand against the Pope and his supporters. After his death, his brother Manfred at first, and later his son Konradin, continued the struggle with the Papacy without much

success. The battles of Benevento in 1266 and Tagliacozzo in 1268 finally saw the end of the Staufer reign in Sicily and the beginning of a rather turbulent period.

The new Papal-sponsored King of Sicily, Charles of Anjou, had to put down severe resistance, especially amongst the Muslims, but by the end of 1270 had consolidated his position. His repressive rule, however, culminated in a revolt on Sicily (known as the Sicilian Vespers) in 1282, giving Pere III of Aragon a pretext to invade Sicily. While the initial invasion was successful on Sicily itself, the Kingdom of Naples remained contested for years, with the war spreading over large parts of the Mediterranean. In mainland Italy it consisted mostly of smaller raids with only few pitched battles, which usually saw the Catalan/Aragonese forces coming out ahead of the Angevins. It also saw the formation and rise of the (in)famous Catalan Company. (See Field of Glory Companion 6: *Eternal Empire*).

Technically King Alfons III of Aragon gave up his claim to Sicily (then ruled by his brother Jaume) with the Treaty of Tarascon (1291), but Jaume and later his son Frederic the Almughavar had enough troops and resources to hold firm even after being deprived of outside assistance. Neither bribes nor force allowed the Angevins to recapture Sicily. The exhausted Charles II gave up all his rights to Sicily in 1302, retaining only the Kingdom of Naples (although that officially kept the name of Kingdom of Sicily, while the kingdom of the actual

Saracen Cavalry

Italo-Norman Nobleman, guardsman and Sicilian levy prisoner, by Angus McBride.
Taken from Elite 9: The Normans

island was called the Kingdom of Trinacria). Afterwards Sicily remained more or less independent until 1409 when it was inherited by the King of Aragon.

TROOP NOTES

Large numbers of Saracen troops were employed. Most were foot bowmen, others were armed with a mixture of javelins, swords, knives, axes and maces. Some wore light mail and some, at least, were "splendidly uniformed". Though large numbers of mounted Saracen archers were employed at times, it is not clear from the sources whether they fought mounted or on foot. Doubt has been cast on their fighting mounted owing to the lack of a mounted archery tradition in western Muslim armies. There are, however, parallels in Andalusia, with locally recruited horse archers being used at least in small numbers. It is also possible that Friedrich II imported horse archer techniques he had seen on Crusade. We therefore allow for the possibility that they fought mounted, and also for the possibility that the bulk of the substantial numbers of Saracen cavalry may have fought in a more traditional North African/Andalusian style.

While there are reports of Friedrich II equipping Saracens 'like knights' we doubt that they actually fought as such. We recommend classifying them as lancer cavalry – for those who disagree the list offers plenty of knights that can be used to represent them.

The Saracens in Italy were completely disarmed under Charles of Anjou and only handed their weapons when enlisted. We assume that lack of practice would render them rather ineffective.

They were finally suppressed by Charles II in 1301.

In the 13th century, most mercenary knights and sergeants were German. The substantial numbers of Catalan-Aragonese knights and cavalls alforrats used by the Aragonese party in Sicily during the War of the Sicilian Vespers can be taken from the normal maxima of Undrilled feudal or mercenary knights.

By the end of the 13th century, Greek troops were relegated to the Arriere-ban.

Almughavars are described as lightly armoured and equipped with a couple of iron darts called sagetes or escones, similar to the Roman pilum or the ancient Spanish soliferrum, a short sword or dagger, and a spear. Their fighting style relied on the effect of missiles combined with a fierce charge. Classification presents a problem – therefore we give a choice of classification. Drilled grading reflects the discipline and training gained after years of continuous service.

Feudal
Sergeant

LATER SICILIAN STARTER ARMY 1225 AD

Commander-in-Chief	1	Field Commander
Sub-commanders	2	2 x Troop Commander
Imperial ministeriales	1 BG	4 bases of Imperial ministeriales: Superior, Heavily Armoured, Drilled Knights – Lancers, Swordsmen
Feudal knights and sergeants	1 BG	6 bases of feudal knights and sergeants: Superior, Heavily Armoured, Undrilled Knights – Lancers, Swordsmen
Saracen cavalry	1 BG	4 bases of Saracen cavalry: Average, Armoured, Drilled Cavalry – Lancers, Swordsmen
Saracen light horse	2 BGs	Each comprising 4 bases of Saracen light horse: Average, Protected, Drilled Light Horse – Javelins, Light Spear
Saracen archers	1 BG	Comprising 8 bases of Saracen archers: Average, Protected, Drilled Medium Foot – Bow
Saracen archers	2 BGs	Each comprising 6 bases of Saracen archers: Average, Unprotected, Drilled Light Foot – Bow
Camp	1	Unfortified camp
Total	8 BGs	Camp, 22 mounted bases, 20 foot bases, 3 commanders

BUILDING A CUSTOMISED LIST USING OUR ARMY POINTS

Choose an army based on the maxima and minima in the list below. The following special instructions apply to this army:

- Commanders should be depicted as knights.
- From 1282 an army must either be that of Sicily or that of Angevin Naples.
- All Medium Foot Almughavars must be classified the same.

LATER SICILIAN

Territory Types: Agricultural, Developed, Hilly

C-in-C		Inspired Commander/Field Commander/Troop Commander					80/50/35	1	
Sub-commanders		Field Commander					50	0–2	
		Troop Commander					35	0–3	
Troop name		Troop Type				Capabilities	Points per base	Bases per BG	Total bases
		Type	Armour	Quality	Training	Shooting	Close Combat		
Core Troops									
Feudal knights and sergeants		Knights	Heavily Armoured	Superior	Undrilled	–	Lancers, Swordsmen	23	4–6	0–24
Mercenary knights and sergeants	Only before 1200	Knights	Heavily Armoured	Superior	Undrilled	–	Lancers, Swordsmen	23	4–6	0–8	6–38
	Only from 1200	Knights	Heavily Armoured	Superior	Undrilled	–	Lancers, Swordsmen	23	4–6	0–20
		Knights	Heavily Armoured	Average	Drilled	–	Lancers, Swordsmen	21	4–6	
Italian Communal knights and sergeants		Knights	Heavily Armoured	Average	Undrilled	–	Lancers, Swordsmen	18	4–6	0–8
Saracen archers	Only before 1267	Light Foot	Unprotected	Average	Drilled or Undrilled	Bow	–	5	6–8	16–36
		Medium Foot	Protected	Average	Drilled	Bow	–	7	6–8	
			Protected		Undrilled			6		
			Unprotected		Drilled			6		
			Unprotected		Undrilled			5		
	Only Angevins from 1267 to 1301	Light Foot	Unprotected	Poor	Undrilled	Bow	–	3	6–8	0–8
		Medium Foot	Unprotected	Poor	Undrilled	Bow	–	3	6–8	

Optional Troops											
Imperial ministeriales	Only from 1215 to 1250	Knights	Heavily Armoured	Superior	Drilled	–	Lancers, Swordsmen	26	4		0–4
Saracen cavalry		Cavalry	Armoured	Superior	Drilled	–	Lancers, Swordsmen	17	4		0–4
				Average	Drilled			13			
				Average	Undrilled			12			
Saracen light horse	Only before 1267	Light Horse	Protected	Average	Drilled or Undrilled	Bow	–	9	4–6	0–8	0–16
		Light Horse	Protected	Average	Drilled or Undrilled	Javelins	Light Spear	8	4–6		
		Light Horse	Unprotected	Average	Drilled or Undrilled	Bow	–	8	4–6	0–16	
		Light Horse	Unprotected	Average	Drilled or Undrilled	Javelins	Light Spear	7	4–6		
Berber light horse		Light Horse	Unprotected	Average	Undrilled	Javelins	Light Spear	7	4–6	0–6	
Feudal, Communal or mercenary spearmen		Heavy Foot	Protected	Average	Undrilled	–	Defensive Spearmen	6	6–8	0–24	0–24
				Average	Drilled			7			
				Poor	Undrilled			4			
				Poor	Drilled			5			
Well equipped mercenary spearmen		Heavy Foot	Armoured	Average	Drilled	–	Defensive Spearmen	9	6–8	0–8	
Greeks	Only before 1200	Medium Foot	Protected	Average	Undrilled	–	Light Spear, Swordsmen	6	6–8	0–16	
		Light Foot	Unprotected	Average	Undrilled	Javelins	Light Spear	4	6–8		
Saracen close fighters	Only before 1267	Heavy Foot or Medium Foot	Armoured	Average	Drilled	–	Light Spear, Swordsmen	9	6–8	0–8	
			Armoured	Average	Undrilled			8			
			Protected	Average	Drilled			7			
			Protected	Average	Undrilled			6			
Communal crossbowmen	Any date	Light Foot	Unprotected	Average	Drilled	Crossbow	–	5	6–8		0–16
				Poor				3			
		Medium Foot	Protected	Average	Drilled	Crossbow	–	7	6–8		
				Poor				5			
	Only from 1200	Heavy Foot	Protected	Average	Drilled	–	Defensive Spearmen	7	1/2	6	0–8
		Medium Foot	Protected	Average	Drilled	Crossbow	–	7	1/2		
		Heavy Foot	Protected	Poor	Drilled	–	Defensive Spearmen	5	1/2	6	0–16
		Medium Foot	Protected	Poor	Drilled	Crossbow	–	5	1/2		
Feudal crossbowmen		Medium Foot	Protected	Average	Undrilled	Crossbow	–	6	6–8	0–8	
Mercenary crossbowmen		Medium Foot	Protected	Average	Drilled	Crossbow	–	7	4–6	0–6	
Catalan crossbowmen	Only Sicily from 1282	Light Foot	Unprotected	Average	Undrilled	Crossbow	–	5	6–8	0–12	
		Medium Foot	Protected	Average	Drilled	Crossbow	–	7	6–8		
					Undrilled			6			
Almughavars	Only Sicily from 1282 to 1291	Medium Foot	Unprotected	Superior	Undrilled	–	Offensive Spearmen	7	6–8	12–36	
			Protected					9			
		Medium Foot	Unprotected	Superior	Undrilled	–	Impact Foot, Swordsmen	7	6–8		
			Protected					9			
	Only Sicily from 1292 to 1301	Medium Foot	Unprotected	Superior	Drilled	–	Offensive Spearmen	8	6–8		
			Protected					10			
		Medium Foot	Unprotected	Superior	Drilled	–	Impact Foot, Swordsmen	8	6–8		
			Protected					10			
Almughavar skirmishers	Only Sicily from 1282 to 1301	Light Foot	Unprotected	Average	Undrilled or Drilled	Javelins	Light Spear	4	4–6	0–6	
Arriere Ban		Mob	Unprotected	Poor	Undrilled	–	–	2	8–12	0–12	
Allies											
Aragonese allies (Only Sicily from 1302)											
Italian Communal allies (Only before 1282)											

EARLY MEDIEVAL IRISH

This list covers native Irish armies from 1167 to 1300.

Forced into exile by the High King Ruaidri Ua Conchobair (Rory O'Connor) in 1166, Diarmait Mac Murchada (Dermot MacMurrough), King of Leinster, fled to the court of Henry II of England, seeking help to regain his kingdom. Granted permission to obtain aid from Henry's vassals, Diarmait secured the interest of several of the Norman lords of Wales, including Richard de Clare, Earl of Pembroke (Strongbow). The first contingent, under Richard fitz Godbert de Roche, arrived in 1167. The main body of Norman, Welsh and Flemish troops arrived in 1169, rapidly gaining control of Leinster, Waterford and Dublin. Strongbow married Diarmait's daughter, and was named heir to the Kingdom of Leinster. Fearing the possible creation of an independent Norman kingdom in Ireland, Henry II arrived with a large fleet in 1171. He declared Waterford and Dublin royal cities, and made his youngest son, John, "Lord of Ireland".

A treaty was signed between Henry and Ruaidri in 1175, leaving Ruaidri as King of the rest of Ireland outside Leinster, Meath, and Waterford, in return for tribute. However, the Norman lords in Ireland did not respect this treaty but continued to expand their lands, advancing far into the west of the island. Throughout the 13th century, however, the policy of the Kings of England was to weaken the power of the Norman lords in Ireland. From the middle of the century onwards, the native Irish began to push back the frontiers of the area under Norman control. This process continued after the end of the period covered by this list, until by the end of the 15th century English control was limited to a relatively small area around Dublin ("The Pale").

TROOP NOTES

Irish warriors of this period were armed with short thrusting spear, javelins and large axes. Although Giraldus Cambrensis describes the Irish axe as used in one hand, several contemporary illustrations, including in his own manuscript, show it being used two-handed. Giraldus states that neither helmet nor mail were any protection against it. "The whole thigh of a soldier, though ever so well cased in iron mail, is cut off by one blow of the axe, the thigh and the leg falling on one side of the horse, and the dying body on the other". We therefore allow players the option to treat all such axes as heavy weapon, or only those used two-handed. In the latter case, battle groups graded as light spear, swordsmen are those with a low proportion of men using two-handed axes.

Armour was rare amongst Irish troops and shields were uncommon.

Skirmishes and ambushes were favoured, but Irish foot sometimes formed up in close order for pitched battle, as at Clontarf before this period.

Bands of landless Irish adventurers hiring themselves out as mercenaries were known in this period as Dibergaigh, as some modelled themselves on the former pagan Diberga and Fianna warrior cults, who shaved their hair at the front and grew it long and plaited at the back.

Following their first employment by Diarmait MacMurchada in 1167, Anglo-Norman mercenaries and allies continued to be found in Irish armies at various times throughout the period. We assume that the

Archer

mercenary leaders were sufficiently independent to be treated as allies.

Galloglaigh (foreign warriors) were mercenary warriors from the Western Isles and west coast of Scotland, serving under their own chieftains. Several clans of galloglaigh settled permanently in Ireland, notably the MacSúibhne (MacSweeney), MacDomhnaill (MacDonnell/MacDowell), MacSiothaigh (MacSheehy), MacDubhgaill (MacDougall), MacCaba (MacCabe) and MacRuari (MacRory) clans. The classic galloglaigh weapon was the two-handed axe, though not all were so armed. They aspired to a mail coat, but grave effigies make it clear that a high proportion wore only a helmet and the textile cotun (akheton).

EARLY MEDIEVAL IRISH STARTER ARMY 1275 AD		
Commander-in-Chief	1	Field Commander
Sub-commanders	2	2 x Troop Commander
Nobles and retainers	1 BG	4 bases of nobles and retainers: Superior, Armoured, Undrilled Cavalry – Light Spear, Swordsmen
Nobles and retainers	2 BGs	Each comprising 4 bases of nobles and retainers: Average, Unprotected, Undrilled Light Horse – Javelins, Light Spear
Galloglaigh	2 BGs	Each comprising 6 bases of galloglaich: Superior, Protected, Undrilled Heavy Foot – Heavy Weapon
Other warriors	4 BGs	Each comprising 8 bases of other warriors: Average, Unprotected, Undrilled Medium Foot – Heavy Weapon
Other warriors	1 BG	6 bases of other warriors: Average, Unprotected, Undrilled Light Foot – Javelins, Light Spear
Levies	3 BGs	Each comprising 6 bases of levies: Poor, Unprotected, Undrilled Light Foot – Javelins, Light Spear
Camp	1	Unfortified camp
Total	13 BGs	Camp, 12 mounted bases, 68 foot bases, 3 commanders

BUILDING A CUSTOMISED LIST USING OUR ARMY POINTS

Choose an army based on the maxima and minima in the list below. The following special instructions apply to this army:

- Commanders should be depicted as nobles and retainers.
- Irish allied commanders' contingents must conform to the Early Medieval Irish allies list below, but the troops in the contingent are deducted from the minima and maxima in the main list.
- Before 1260 nobles and retainers upgraded to cavalry can always dismount as Medium Foot, Unprotected, Superior, Undrilled, Heavy Weapon.
- The minima marked * only apply if any Anglo-Norman troops are used.

EARLY MEDIEVAL IRISH

Territory Types: Agricultural, Hilly, Woodlands

C-in-C	Inspired Commander/Field Commander/Troop Commander					80/50/35		1	
Sub-commanders	Field Commander/Troop Commander					50/35		0–2	
Irish allied commanders	Field Commander/Troop Commander					40/25		0–2	

Troop name		Troop Type				Capabilities		Points per base	Bases per BG	Total bases
		Type	Armour	Quality	Training	Shooting	Close Combat			
Core Troops										
Nobles and retainers	Any date	Medium or Heavy Foot	Unprotected	Superior	Undrilled	–	Heavy Weapon	7	6–8	0–16	6–16
	Only before 1260	Cavalry	Protected	Average	Undrilled	–	Light Spear, Swordsmen	9	4–6	0–16	
	Only from 1260	Cavalry	Armoured	Superior	Undrilled	–	Light Spear, Swordsmen	16	4	0–4	
		Light Horse	Unprotected	Average	Undrilled	Javelins	Light Spear	7	4–6	4–10	
Other warriors		Medium Foot	Unprotected	Average	Undrilled	–	Heavy Weapon	6	6–8	24–120	
		Medium Foot	Unprotected	Average	Undrilled	–	Light Spear, Swordsmen	5	6–8		
		Light Foot	Unprotected	Average	Undrilled	Javelins	Light Spear	4	6–8	6–40	
Optional Troops										
Dibergaigh		Medium Foot	Unprotected	Superior	Undrilled	–	Heavy Weapon	7	6–8	0–8	
Galloglaigh	Only from 1260	Heavy Foot	Protected	Superior	Undrilled	–	Heavy Weapon	9	6–8	0–12	
				Average				7			
Levies		Light Foot	Unprotected	Poor	Undrilled	Javelins	Light Spear	2	6–8	0–36	
Slingers		Light Foot	Unprotected	Average	Undrilled	Sling	–	4	4–6	0–6	
Archers		Light Foot	Unprotected	Average	Undrilled	Bow	–	5	4–6		
Trenches, abatis or plashing		Field Fortifications						3		0–24	
Fortified Camp								24		0–1	
Allies										

Anglo–Norman allies – Early Anglo–Irish

Islesmen allies (Only from 1200) – Early Scots Isles and Highlands

Viking or Ostmen allies (Only before 1195) – Viking – See Field of Glory Companion 8: *Wolves from the Sea: The Dark Ages*

EARLY MEDIEVAL IRISH ALLIES

Allied commander		Field Commander/Troop Commander						40/25		1	
Troop name		Troop Type				Capabilities		Points per base	Bases per BG	Total bases	
		Type	Armour	Quality	Training	Shooting	Close Combat				
Nobles and retainers	Any date	Medium or Heavy Foot	Unprotected	Superior	Undrilled	–	Heavy Weapon	7	4–6	0–6	4–6
	Only before 1260	Cavalry	Protected	Average	Undrilled	–	Light Spear, Swordsmen	9	4–6	0–6	
	Only from 1260	Light Horse	Unprotected	Average	Undrilled	Javelins	Light Spear	7	4	0–4	
Other warriors		Medium Foot	Unprotected	Average	Undrilled	–	Heavy Weapon	6	6–8	8–32	
		Medium Foot	Unprotected	Average	Undrilled	–	Light Spear, Swordsmen	5	6–8		
		Light Foot	Unprotected	Average	Undrilled	Javelins	Light Spear	4	6–8	0–12	
Galloglaigh	Only from 1260	Heavy Foot	Protected	Superior	Undrilled	–	Heavy Weapon	9	4	0–4	
				Average				7			
Levies		Light Foot	Unprotected	Poor	Undrilled	Javelins	Light Spear	2	6–8	0–12	

Irish troops ambush Anglo-Irish knight, by Angus McBride. Taken from Elite 9: The Normans

EARLY ANGLO-IRISH

This list covers Anglo-Irish armies from 1172 to 1300, and Anglo-Irish mercenary or allied contingents from 1167 to 1300.

TROOP NOTES

Scots colonists from the Western seaboard of Scotland were settled in northern Ulster following grants of land to the Earls of Galloway and Atholl by King John.

Large armies usually included Irish allied contingents.

English
Knight

EARLY ANGLO-IRISH STARTER ARMY 1275 AD

Commander-in-Chief	1	Field Commander
Sub-commanders	2	2 x Troop Commander
Knights and sergeants	2 BGs	Each comprising 4 bases of knights and sergeants: Superior, Heavily Armoured, Undrilled Knights – Lancers, Swordsmen
Foot sergeants	1 BG	8 bases of foot sergeants: Average, Protected, Undrilled Heavy Foot – Defensive Spearmen
Welsh or English archers	2 BGs	Each comprising 8 bases of Welsh or English archers: Average, Protected, Undrilled Medium Foot – Longbow, Swordsmen
Irish warriors	2 BGs	Each comprising 8 bases of Irish warriors: Average, Unprotected, Undrilled Medium Foot – Heavy Weapon
Irish warriors	2 BGs	Each comprising 6 bases of Irish warriors: Poor, Unprotected, Undrilled Light Foot – Javelins, Light Spear
Camp	1	Unfortified camp
Total	9 BGs	Camp, 8 mounted bases, 52 foot bases, 3 commanders

BUILDING A CUSTOMISED LIST USING OUR ARMY POINTS

Choose an army based on the maxima and minima in the list below. The following special instructions apply to this army:

- Commanders should be depicted as knights.
- Anglo-Irish allied commanders' contingents must conform to the Anglo-Irish allies list below, but the troops in the contingent are deducted from the minima and maxima in the main list.

English Archer

EARLY ANGLO-IRISH

Territory Types: Agricultural

C-in-C	Inspired Commander/Field Commander/Troop Commander				80/50/35		1
Sub-commanders	Field Commander/Troop Commander				50/35		0–2
Anglo–Irish allied commanders	Field Commander/Troop Commander				40/25		0–2

Troop name	Troop Type				Capabilities		Points per base	Bases per BG	Total bases
	Type	Armour	Quality	Training	Shooting	Close Combat			
Core Troops									
Norman knights and sergeants	Knights	Heavily Armoured	Superior	Undrilled	–	Lancers, Swordsmen	23	4–6	4–12 / 4–12
Knights and sergeants with lighter equipment	Cavalry	Armoured	Average	Undrilled	–	Lancers, Swordsmen	12	4	0–4
Separately deployed hobilars	Only from 1290	Cavalry	Protected	Average	Undrilled	–	Lancers, Swordsmen	9	4–6	4–8
Foot sergeants	Heavy Foot	Protected	Average	Undrilled	–	Defensive Spearmen	6	6–8	6–24
Welsh archers	Any date	Medium Foot	Unprotected	Average	Undrilled	Longbow	–	6	6–8	0–32 / 8–32
English archers	Only before 1275	Light Foot	Unprotected	Average	Undrilled	Bow	–	5	6–8	0–8
		Medium Foot	Unprotected	Average	Undrilled	Bow	–	5	6–8	
Welsh or English archers	Only from 1275	Medium Foot	Protected	Average	Undrilled	Longbow	Swordsmen	8	6–8	8–32
			Unprotected					7		
		Medium Foot	Protected	Average	Undrilled	Longbow		7	6–8	
			Unprotected					6		
Irish warriors		Medium Foot	Unprotected	Average	Undrilled	–	Heavy Weapon	6	6–8	8–36 / 8–40
		Medium Foot	Unprotected	Average	Undrilled	–	Light Spear, Swordsmen	5	6–8	
		Light Foot	Unprotected	Average	Undrilled	Javelins	Light Spear	4	6–8	0–12
				Poor				2		
Optional Troops									
Mercenary crossbowmen	Medium Foot	Protected	Average	Drilled	Crossbow	–	7	4	0–4
Irish archers	Light Foot	Unprotected	Average	Undrilled	Bow	–	5	4	0–4
Ostmen	Heavy Foot	Protected	Average	Undrilled	–	Heavy Weapon	7	6–8	0–8 / 0–12
	Heavy Foot	Protected	Average	Undrilled	–	Offensive Spearmen	7	6–8	
Scots colonists	Only from 1212	Heavy Foot	Protected	Average	Undrilled	–	Heavy Weapon	7	6–8	0–12
		Heavy Foot	Protected	Average	Undrilled	–	Offensive Spearmen	7	6–8	
Allies									

Irish allies – Early Medieval Irish (Up to 2 contingents)

Manx Viking allies (Only from 1177 to 1266) – Viking – See Field of Glory Companion 8: *Wolves from the Sea: The Dark Ages*

EARLY ANGLO–IRISH ALLIES

Allied commander		Field Commander/Troop Commander						40/25	1	
Troop name		**Troop Type**				**Capabilities**		Points per base	Bases per BG	Total bases
		Type	Armour	Quality	Training	Shooting	Close Combat			
Norman knights and sergeants		Knights	Heavily Armoured	Superior	Undrilled	–	Lancers, Swordsmen	23	4	0–4
Separately deployed hobilars	Only from 1290	Cavalry	Protected	Average	Undrilled	–	Lancers, Swordsmen	9	4	0–4
Foot sergeants		Heavy Foot	Protected	Average	Undrilled	–	Defensive Spearmen	6	4–6	0–6
Welsh archers	Any date	Medium Foot	Unprotected	Average	Undrilled	Longbow	–	6	4–8	4–8
Welsh or English archers	Only from 1275	Medium Foot	Protected	Average	Undrilled	Longbow	Swordsmen	8	4–8	4–8
			Unprotected					7		
		Medium Foot	Protected	Average	Undrilled	Longbow	–	7	4–8	
			Unprotected					6		
Irish warriors	Only from 1172	Medium Foot	Unprotected	Average	Undrilled	–	Heavy Weapon	6	6–8	0–8	0–12
		Medium Foot	Unprotected	Average	Undrilled	–	Light Spear, Swordsmen	5	6–8	
		Light Foot	Unprotected	Average	Undrilled	Javelins	Light Spear	4	4	0–4
				Poor				2		

EARLY TEUTONIC KNIGHTS

The Teutonic Knights or Teutonic Order (The Order of the German House of St. Mary in Jerusalem) was founded as a German hospital order during the siege of Acre in 1190 and transformed into a military order in 1198. The Teutonic Order never managed to become as powerful and famous in Outremer as the Templars or Hospitallers. Its true calling was found in Eastern Europe where the Order expanded greatly during the 13th century.

In 1211 King Andrew II of Hungary accepted the aid of the Knights in defending Hungary against the Cumans, granting them lands in the Burzenland in Siebenbürgen (Transylvania). This offer was probably a result of negotiations for the marriage of his daughter with the son of Hermann, Landgrave of Thuringia, as the family of the Order's Grand Master, Hermann von Salza, were the Landgrave's vassals. In the years that followed the Order successfully defended Hungary against Cuman raids, but also invited more German colonists to settle among those already present (the so called Siebenbürger Saxons). Finally, in 1224, the Order sent a petition to Pope Honorius III, asking to be placed under direct Papal authority. This would have resulted in an Ordenstaat independent of the Kings of Hungary. King Andrew could not tolerate this and expelled the Knights from Hungary in 1225.

Even before that the German Emperor Friedrich II had already elevated his close friend von Salza to the

Teutonic Commander

status of Reichsfürst, or "Prince of the Empire", allowing the Grand Master to negotiate with other senior princes as an equal. He also permitted the Grand Master to add the Imperial Eagle to his standard and encouraged von Salza to become active in the Baltic area.

In 1226 Konrad I, Duke of Masovia in west-central Poland, invited the Teutonic Knights to assist in the conquest of the pagan Prussians, granting them and the Order of Dobrzyń (which Konrad had founded) the use of the Kulmerland (Chełmno Land) in modern central Poland as their base. In the same year Emperor Friedrich II bestowed special rights on the Order for the conquest and possession of Prussia, including Chełmno Land, with nominal Papal sovereignty. In 1235 the Teutonic Knights assimilated the smaller Order of Dobrzyń. The following year they also absorbed the Schwertbrüder Orden (Livonian Brothers of the Sword) – which had been founded in 1202 and operated around the Gulf of Riga – following the severe defeat of the Schwertbrüder by the Lithuanians and Semigallians at the Battle of Schaulen (Saule).

In 1242 there was the famous clash between the Teutonic Order and the Republic of Novgorod, the so-called "Battle of Lake Peipus". Despite long established Russian tradition, however, there is nothing to suggest it was more than a small and rather unimportant skirmish.

Taking advantage of the current crusading atmosphere as well as the general boredom many nobles faced during the winter months, the Order soon started to organize annual 'winter crusades' into the territories they were trying to capture. With this added manpower the Order managed to slowly but surely subdue the natives over a period of almost 50 years. After the Prussians were finally subdued the Order then began to expand into Livonia. By 1300 the Teutonic Order was well established in Prussia, Latvia, Estonia, and Livonia.

This list covers the armies of the Teutonic Orders from 1202 to 1300.

TROOP NOTES

Subject foot included Estonians, Kurs, Letts, Livs and Prussians. (We assume that Slavic foot during the Hungarian period would be similar). Turcopoles were mercenary or native light cavalry. We have found no evidence for the horse archers included in previous published army lists.

EARLY TEUTONIC KNIGHTS STARTER ARMY 1250 AD

Commander-in-Chief	1	Field Commander
Sub-commanders	2	2 x Troop Commander
Brother knights and sergeants	2 BGs	Each comprising 4 bases of brother knights and sergeants: Superior, Heavily Armoured, Drilled Knights – Lancers, Swordsmen
Other knights and sergeants	1 BG	4 bases of other knights and sergeants: Superior, Heavily Armoured, Undrilled Knights – Lancers, Swordsmen
Turcopoles	3 BGs	Each comprising 4 bases of turcopoles: Average, Unprotected, Undrilled Light Horse – Javelins, Light Spear
Serving brother spearmen	1 BG	6 bases of serving brother spearmen: Average, Armoured, Drilled Heavy Foot – Defensive Spearmen
Serving brother crossbowmen	1 BG	6 bases of serving brother crossbowmen: Average, Protected, Drilled Medium Foot – Crossbow
Camp	1	Unfortified camp
Total	8 BGs	Camp, 24 mounted bases, 12 foot bases, 3 commanders

BUILDING A CUSTOMISED LIST USING OUR ARMY POINTS

Choose an army based on the maxima and minima in the list below. The following special instructions apply to this army:

- Commanders should be depicted as brother knights.

- The minima marked * apply if any troops so marked are used.
- Knights can always dismount as Superior, Heavily Armoured, Drilled or Undrilled (as mounted type) Heavy Foot – Heavy Weapon.

Dismounted Brother Knight

EARLY TEUTONIC KNIGHTS

Territory Types: Agricultural, Woodlands. Only from 1211 to 1225 – Hilly

C-in-C		Inspired Commander/Field Commander/Troop Commander					80/50/35		1	
Sub-commanders		Field Commander					50		0–2	
		Troop Commander					35		0–3	

Troop name		Troop Type				Capabilities		Points per base	Bases per BG	Total bases	
		Type	Armour	Quality	Training	Shooting	Close Combat				
Core Troops											
Brother knights and sergeants		Knights	Heavily Armoured	Superior	Drilled	–	Lancers, Swordsmen	26	4–6	4–12	
Vassal, "Crusader" or mercenary men–at–arms		Knights	Heavily Armoured	Superior	Undrilled	–	Lancers, Swordsmen	23	4–6	0–16	Before 1230 0–8, From 1230 4–16
		Knights	Heavily Armoured	Average	Drilled	–	Lancers, Swordsmen	21	4–6	0–12	
Turcopoles	Only from 1230	Light Horse	Unprotected	Average	Undrilled	Javelins	Light Spear	7	4–6	4–12	
		Cavalry	Protected	Average	Undrilled	–	Light Spear, Swordsmen	9	4–6		
Serving brother or mercenary spearmen		Heavy Foot	Armoured	Average	Drilled	–	Defensive Spearmen	9	4–6	*4–6	
			Protected					7			
Serving brother or mercenary crossbowmen		Medium Foot	Protected	Average	Drilled	Crossbow	–	7	6–8	*6–12	
Subject foot spearmen		Heavy Foot	Protected	Average	Undrilled	–	Defensive Spearmen	6	6–8	0–8	
				Poor				4			
		Medium Foot	Protected	Average	Undrilled	–	Light Spear	5	6–8	0–16	
				Poor				3			
Subject foot archers		Light Foot	Unprotected	Average	Undrilled	Bow	–	5	6–8	0–8	
				Poor				3			
Optional Troops											
Mounted crossbowmen		Cavalry	Armoured	Average	Drilled	Crossbow	Swordsmen	14	4–6	0–6	
Hungarians	Only from 1211 to 1225	Light Horse	Unprotected	Average	Undrilled	Bow	–	8	4–6	0–8	
		Light Horse	Unprotected	Average	Undrilled	Bow	Swordsmen	10	4–6		
German town militia spearmen		Heavy Foot	Protected	Average	Drilled	–	Defensive Spearmen	7	6–8	0–12	
				Average	Undrilled			6			
				Poor	Drilled			5			
				Poor	Undrilled			4			
German town militia crossbowmen		Medium Foot	Protected	Average	Drilled	Crossbow	–	7	6–8	0–8	
				Average	Undrilled			6			
				Poor	Drilled			5			
				Poor	Undrilled			4			
Vassal or "Crusader" crossbowmen		Medium Foot	Protected	Average	Undrilled	Crossbow	–	6	6–8		
Allies											
Polish allies (Only from 1226 to 1242) – Feudal Polish											

Teutonic Knights in Cumania, by Graham Turner. Taken from Warrior 124: Teutonic Knight

EARLY TEUTONIC KNIGHTS ALLIES

Allied commander		Field Commander/Troop Commander						40/25		1	
Troop name		Troop Type				Capabilities		Points per base	Bases per BG	Total bases	
		Type	Armour	Quality	Training	Shooting	Close Combat				
Brother knights and sergeants		Knights	Heavily Armoured	Superior	Drilled	–	Lancers, Swordsmen	26	4	4	
Vassal, "Crusader" or mercenary men-at-arms	Only from 1230	Knights	Heavily Armoured	Superior	Undrilled	–	Lancers, Swordsmen	23	4–6	0–6	4–6
		Knights	Heavily Armoured	Average	Drilled	–	Lancers, Swordsmen	21	4–6	0–4	
Turcopoles	Only from 1230	Light horse	Unprotected	Average	Undrilled	Javelins	Light Spear	7	4		0–4
		Cavalry	Protected	Average	Undrilled	–	Light Spear, Swordsmen	9	4		
Serving brother or mercenary crossbowmen		Medium Foot	Protected	Average	Drilled	Crossbow	–	7	4	0–4	
Subject foot spearmen		Medium Foot	Protected	Average	Undrilled	–	Light Spear	5	4–6	0–6	
				Poor				3			

MONGOL INVASION

This list covers the Mongol armies that invaded Russia and Europe from 1223 to 1242.

In 1223 a Kievan Russian army, with Cuman allies, was defeated at the Kalka River by a Mongol reconnaissance force under Subutai..

After the death of Ghengis Khan in 1227, command of the Mongol forces in South Russia was divided between Ghengis's grandsons, the brothers Batu in the west (Blue Horde) and Orda in the east (White Horde). Batu had the larger forces, mostly recruited from conquered tribes, including Cumans (Polovtsy), Alans, Bashkirs, Burtas, Circassians, Karburdians, Kirghiz, Khwarazmians, Mordvins, Volga Bulgars and others.

Between 1236 and 1239, Batu's forces subjugated the Volga Bulgars and the Russian principalities. Most of the latter retained vassal status rather than being directly incorporated into the Horde's territories.

In 1241 Mongol forces invaded Central Europe. Batu's forces (under the supreme command of the Great Khan's general Subutai) invaded Hungary, while Orda's forces invaded Poland. The Hungarians were severely defeated at Mohi and the Poles at Legnicą (Liegnitz). Fortunately for Europe, the Great Khan, Ögedei, died the same year, and the Mongol leaders broke off the campaign to take part in the election of a new Great Khan.

After his return in 1242, Batu established his capital at Sarai, on the lower Volga. Following Batu's death in 1255, the Blue and White Hordes were consolidated into a single state by Batu's brother and successor, Berke. This state came to be known as the Golden Horde, and was the longest lasting of the Mongol successor states. "Tatar" came to be the general term used for its multi-ethnic population. Its armies are covered by the Tatar list in Field of Glory Companion 6: *Eternal Empire*.

TROOP NOTES

Mongol cavalry include troops raised from subjugated tribes and trained to Mongol standards.

MONGOL INVASION STARTER ARMY		
Commander-in-Chief	1	Inspired Commander (Subutai)
Sub-commanders	2	2 x Troop Commander
Guard cavalry	1 BG	4 bases of guard cavalry: Elite, Armoured, Drilled Cavalry – Bow, Swordsmen
Best equipped cavalry	1 BG	4 bases of best equipped cavalry: Superior, Armoured, Drilled Cavalry – Bow, Swordsmen
Other Mongol cavalry	2 BGs	Each comprising 4 bases of other Mongol cavalry: Superior, Protected, Drilled Cavalry – Bow, Swordsmen
Other Mongol cavalry	4 BGs	Each comprising 4 bases of other Mongol cavalry: Average, Unprotected, Drilled Light Horse – Bow, Swordsmen
Camp	1	Unfortified camp
Total	8 BGs	Camp, 32 mounted bases, 3 commanders

Mongol heavy cavalryman, by Angus McBride. Taken from Men-at-Arms 105: The Mongols

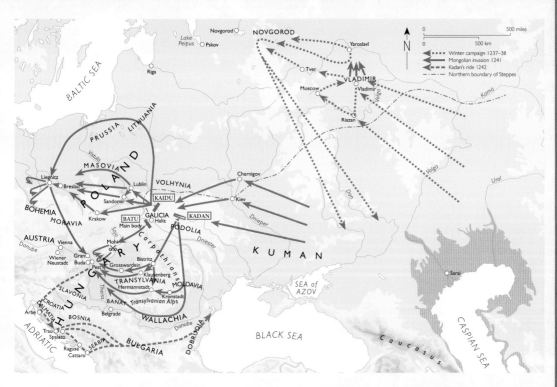

The Mongol Invasion of Europe. Taken from Essential Histories 57: Genghis Khan & the Mongol
Conquests 1190–1400

BUILDING A CUSTOMISED LIST USING OUR ARMY POINTS

Choose an army based on the maxima and
minima in the list below. The following special
instructions apply to this army:

- Commanders should be depicted as guard
  or best equipped Mongol cavalry.

- Mongol cavalry can always dismount. Light
  Horse dismount as Light Foot, Cavalry as
  Medium Foot. Armour, quality, training, and
  shooting and close combat capabilities are
  the same as when mounted.

MONGOL INVASION

Territory Types: Steppes

C-in-C	Inspired Commander/Field Commander/Troop Commander					80/50/35		1
Sub-commanders	Field Commander					50		0–2
	Troop Commander					35		0–3

Troop name	Troop Type				Capabilities		Points per base	Bases per BG	Total bases
	Type	Armour	Quality	Training	Shooting	Close Combat			
Core Troops									
Guard cavalry	Cavalry	Armoured	Elite	Drilled	Bow	Swordsmen	22	4	0–4
Best equipped Mongol cavalry	Cavalry	Armoured	Superior	Drilled	Bow	Swordsmen	19	4–6	4–16
Other Mongol cavalry	Light Horse	Unprotected	Superior	Drilled	Bow	Swordsmen	12	4–6	16–60
			Average				10		
	Cavalry	Unprotected	Superior	Drilled	Bow	Swordsmen	13	4–6	
		Unprotected	Average				11		
		Protected	Superior				15		
		Protected	Average				12		
Optional Troops									
Other nomad cavalry	Light Horse	Unprotected	Average	Undrilled	Bow	Swordsmen	10	4–6	0–36
	Cavalry	Unprotected	Average	Undrilled	Bow	Swordsmen	10	4–6	
		Protected					11		
Stone throwers and bolt shooters	Heavy Artillery	–	Average	Drilled	Heavy Artillery	–	20	2	0–4
Fortified Camp							24		0–1

EARLY GRANADINE

Muhammed I ibn Nasr, founder of the Nasrid dynasty, became the effectively independent Emir of Granada (in the far south of modern Spain) in 1232 AD after the departure of the last Almohad prince, Idris, from Iberia to take the Almohad leadership in North Africa. The Nasrids initially aligned themselves with Castile, Granada becoming a tributary state and officially a kingdom in 1238. Prior to the Almoravid conquest, Granada had been a Taifa kingdom from 1013 to 1090.

Granada adopted the political structure of the Cordova Caliphate, and came to be a cultural and economic power (the famous Alhambra palace in Granada was built by the Nasrids), but was forced to pay tribute to the Christian kingdoms to avoid being attacked.

The Marinid Berbers of North Africa supported the Kingdom of Granada. Thanks to the strength of the Granadine and Marinid fleets, the Christians were forced to attack by land across Granada's strongly fortified and mountainous borders.

This list covers the armies of Granada from 1232 to 1340. Following the defeat of the combined Marinid and Granadine army at the Battle of Rio Salado that year, the Christians took control of the Straits of Gibraltar, and

Mercenary Spearman

Granada was isolated from North Africa. The later armies of Granada, until the fall of the kingdom to the Spanish in 1492, are covered by the Later Granadine list in Field of Glory Companion 2: *Storm of Arrows*.

TROOP NOTES

In this period Granadine heavy cavalry were equipped and fought like Christian knights. They wore full mail armour, helmets – sometimes barrel-helms adapted to accommodate a turban – and mail horse barding. Some, indeed, were Christians captured in youth and brought up in the Islamic faith but trained and armed in the Christian manner. Christian mercenary knights were also used.

"Ghuzz" mercenaries were used on the borders. Camelry were initially supplied by the Marinids, but later adopted into the Granadine army, as depicted in the "King's Room" in the Alhambra which shows camels ridden by riders with long lances.

EARLY GRANADINE STARTER ARMY 1275 AD		
Commander-in-Chief	1	Field Commander
Sub-commanders	2	2 x Troop Commander
Granadine lancers	2 BGs	Each comprising 4 bases of Granadine lancers: Superior, Heavily Armoured, Drilled Knights – Lancers, Swordsmen
Granadine and Berber cavalry	3 BGs	Each comprising 4 bases of Granadine and Berber cavalry: Average, Unprotected, Drilled Light Horse – Javelins, Light Spear
Town militia or mercenary spearmen	2 BGs	Each comprising 6 bases of spearmen: Average, Protected, Drilled Heavy Foot –Defensive Spearmen
Peasant archers	2 BGs	Each comprising 6 bases of archers: Average, Unprotected, Undrilled Light Foot – Bow
Peasant crossbowmen	1 BG	8 bases of crossbowmen: Average, Unprotected, Undrilled Light Foot – Crossbow
Camp	1	Unfortified camp
Total	10 BGs	Camp, 20 mounted bases, 32 foot bases, 3 commanders

BUILDING A CUSTOMISED LIST USING OUR ARMY POINTS

Choose an army based on the maxima and minima in the list below. The following special instructions apply to this army:

- Commanders should be depicted as Granadine lancers or Granadine cavalry.
- Christian mercenary knights cannot be used with camelry or Berber javelinmen, nor with Marinid allies.

Border Soldier

EARLY GRANADINE

Territory Types: Agricultural, Developed, Mountains

C-in-C	Inspired Commander/Field Commander/Troop Commander					80/50/35	1	
Sub-commanders	Field Commander					50	0–2	
	Troop Commander					35	0–3	

Troop name	Troop Type				Capabilities		Points per base	Bases per BG	Total bases
	Type	Armour	Quality	Training	Shooting	Close Combat			
Core Troops									
Granadine lancers	Knights	Heavily Armoured	Superior	Drilled	–	Lancers, Swordsmen	26	4–6	4–8
Granadine and Berber cavalry	Light Horse	Unprotected	Average	Drilled	Javelins	Light Spear	7	4–6	8–24
Town militia or mercenary spearmen	Heavy Foot	Protected	Average	Drilled	–	Defensive Spearmen	7	6–8	6–24
			Poor				5		
Peasant archers and crossbowmen	Light Foot	Unprotected	Average	Undrilled	Bow	–	5	6–8	12–64
			Poor				3		
	Medium Foot	Unprotected	Average	Undrilled	Bow	–	5	6–8	
			Poor				3		
	Light Foot	Unprotected	Average	Undrilled	Crossbow	–	5	6–8	
			Poor				3		
	Medium Foot	Unprotected	Average	Undrilled	Crossbow	–	5	6–8	
			Poor				3		
Optional Troops									
Horse archers	Light Horse	Unprotected	Average	Drilled	Bow	–	8	4–6	0–6
Mounted crossbowmen	Light Horse	Unprotected	Average	Drilled	Crossbow	–	7	4–6	
Christian mercenary knights	Knights	Heavily armoured	Superior	Undrilled	–	Lancers, Swordsmen	23	4	0–4
Camelry	Camelry	Protected	Average	Undrilled	–	Lancers, Swordsmen	11	4–6	0–6
"Ghuzz" mercenaries	Light Horse	Unprotected	Average	Undrilled	Bow	Swordsmen	10	4	0–4
	Cavalry	Unprotected	Average	Undrilled	Bow	Swordsmen	10	4	
		Protected					11		
Border soldiers	Medium Foot	Protected	Average	Undrilled	–	Light Spear	5	6–8	0–8
Mercenary or town militia crossbowmen	Medium Foot	Protected	Average	Drilled	Crossbow	–	7	4–6	0–8
			Poor				5		
Mercenary archers	Medium Foot	Protected	Average	Drilled	Bow	–	7	4–6	
		Unprotected					6		
Slingers	Light Foot	Unprotected	Average	Undrilled	Sling	–	4	4–6	0–6
Berber javelinmen	Light Foot	Unprotected	Average	Undrilled	Javelins	Light Spear	4	6–8	0–12
Allies									

Marinid allies – Fanatic Berber

EARLY GRANADINE ALLIES

Allied commander	Field Commander/Troop Commander						40/25	1	
Troop name	Troop Type				Capabilities		Points per base	Bases per BG	Total bases
	Type	Armour	Quality	Training	Shooting	Close Combat			
Granadine lancers	Knights	Heavily Armoured	Superior	Drilled	–	Lancers, Swordsmen	26	4	0–4
Granadine and Berber cavalry	Light Horse	Unprotected	Average	Drilled	Javelins	Light Spear	7	4–6	4–8
Town militia or mercenary spearmen	Heavy Foot	Protected	Average	Drilled	–	Defensive Spearmen	7	6–8	0–8
			Poor				5		
Peasant archers and crossbowmen	Light Foot	Unprotected	Average	Undrilled	Bow	–	5	6–8	6–18
			Poor				3		
	Medium Foot	Unprotected	Average	Undrilled	Bow	–	5	6–8	
			Poor				3		
	Light Foot	Unprotected	Average	Undrilled	Crossbow	–	5	6–8	
			Poor				3		
	Medium Foot	Unprotected	Average	Undrilled	Crossbow	–	5	6–8	
			Poor				3		

MIDDLE PLANTAGENET ENGLISH

Edward I ascended the throne in 1272 AD following the death of his father Henry III. In 1276 he invaded Wales, conquered most of the country and left Llywelyn ap Gruffydd with only a rump of Gwynedd. A rebellion in 1282 collapsed following the death of Llywelyn. In 1284 Wales was incorporated into England under the Statute of Rhuddlan.

Following the death of the Scots King Alexander III in 1286, there was no direct male heir to the throne. Edward succeeded in betrothing his heir, Edward of Caernarfon, to Alexander's granddaughter Margaret (daughter of King Eirik II of Norway), but she died on the way from Norway to take the Scottish throne. To prevent civil war, the Scottish Guardians invited Edward to arbitrate between the rival claimants to the throne. He did so, but only on condition that he be recognised as Overlord of Scotland. King John Balliol was crowned in November 1292, but Edward continued to undermine Scottish independence. In 1296 Edward invaded, and deposed King John. The First Scottish

War of Independence followed, lasting until Edward III finally recognised Scottish independence in 1328.

Edward also fought wars with Philip IV of France from 1294 to 1298 and 1300 to 1303. He died in 1307, and was succeeded by his son Edward. Edward II was a weak king, during whose reign Scotland was reconquered by King Robert the Bruce. He was deposed in 1327, in favour of his 14-year old son Edward III, and murdered later the same year.

This list covers English armies from 1272 to 1320.

TROOP NOTES

The main characteristic feature of English armies of this period was the fielding of large numbers of longbowmen. This seems to have been an innovation by King Edward I following his Welsh wars. Initially most of the longbowmen were Welsh, but later in the period the longbow also became the main weapon of the English yeomanry. All freemen with 40–100s worth of

land were expected to serve with bow and sword, those with less with bow and whatever hand-to-hand weapons they could get, including knives, pole-arms such as gisarmes and fauchards and assorted peasant weapons. Most wore quilted gambesons (aketons).

By this time the decline of the feudal system had drastically reduced the size of feudal knightly contingents, the shortfall being made up with paid mercenaries.

English Archer

MIDDLE PLANTAGENET ENGLISH STARTER ARMY 1285 AD		
Commander-in-Chief	1	Field Commander
Sub-commanders	2	2 x Troop Commander
Royal household knights and sergeants	1 BG	2 bases of royal household knights and sergeants: Superior, Heavily Armoured, Drilled Knights – Lancers, Swordsmen
Feudal knights and sergeants	2 BGs	Each comprising 4 bases of feudal knights and sergeants: Superior, Heavily Armoured, Undrilled Knights – Lancers, Swordsmen
Spearmen	1 BG	8 bases of spearmen: Average, Protected, Undrilled Heavy Foot – Defensive Spearmen
Welsh or English archers	4 BGs	Each comprising 6 bases of Welsh or English archers: Average, Protected, Undrilled Medium Foot – Longbow, Swordsmen
Camp	1	Unfortified camp
Total	8 BGs	Camp, 10 mounted bases, 32 foot bases, 3 commanders

BUILDING A CUSTOMISED LIST USING OUR ARMY POINTS

Choose an army based on the maxima and minima in the list below. The following special instructions apply to this army:

Spearman

- Commanders should be depicted as knights.
- No more than one allied contingent can be used.

MIDDLE PLANTAGENET ENGLISH

Territory Types: Agricultural, Woodlands

C-in-C	Inspired Commander/Field Commander/Troop Commander					80/50/35	1	
Sub-commanders	Field Commander					50	0–2	
	Troop Commander					35	0–3	

Troop name	Troop Type				Capabilities		Points per base	Bases per BG	Total bases
	Type	Armour	Quality	Training	Shooting	Close Combat			
Core Troops									
Royal household knights and sergeants	Knights	Heavily Armoured	Superior	Drilled	–	Lancers, Swordsmen	26	2	0–2	6–24
Feudal knights and sergeants	Knights	Heavily Armoured	Superior	Undrilled	–	Lancers, Swordsmen	23	4–6	4–18
Mercenary knights and sergeants	Knights	Heavily Armoured	Superior	Undrilled	–	Lancers, Swordsmen	23	4–6	0–8
	Knights	Heavily Armoured	Average	Drilled	–	Lancers, Swordsmen	21	4–6	
Spearmen	Heavy Foot	Protected	Average	Undrilled	–	Defensive Spearmen	6	6–8	0–16	0–16
	Heavy Foot	Protected	Poor	Undrilled	–	Defensive Spearmen	4	6–8	
	Heavy Foot	Protected	Average	Drilled	–	Defensive Spearmen	7	6–8	0–8
	Heavy Foot	Protected	Poor	Drilled	–	Defensive Spearmen	5	6–8	0–12
Welsh or English archers	Medium Foot	Protected	Average	Undrilled	Longbow	Swordsmen	8	6–8	8–60
	Medium Foot	Unprotected	Average	Undrilled	Longbow	Swordsmen	7	6–8	
	Medium Foot	Protected	Average	Undrilled	Longbow	–	7	6–8	
	Medium Foot	Unprotected	Average	Undrilled	Longbow	–	6	6–8	
Optional Troops									
Separately deployed sergeants	Cavalry	Armoured	Average	Undrilled	–	Lancers, Swordsmen	12	4–6	0–6
Mounted crossbowmen	Cavalry	Armoured	Average	Undrilled	Crossbow	Swordsmen	13	4	0–4
Gascon crossbowmen	Medium Foot	Protected	Average	Undrilled	Crossbow	–	6	6–8	0–16
Irish foot — Only in Britain or Ireland	Medium Foot	Unprotected	Average	Undrilled	–	Heavy Weapon	6	4–6	0–6
	Medium Foot	Unprotected	Average	Undrilled	–	Light Spear, Swordsmen	5	4–6	
	Light Foot	Unprotected	Average	Undrilled	Javelins	Light Spear	4	4–6	
Allies									
Irish allies – Early Medieval Irish									
North Welsh allies – Later Welsh									

Longbowmen, by Gerry Embleton. Taken from *Warrior 11: English Longbowman 1330–1515*

APPENDIX 1 – USING THE LISTS

To give balanced games, armies can be selected using the points system. The more effective the troops, the more each base costs in points. The maximum points for an army will usually be set at between 600 and 800 points for a singles game for 2 to 4 hours play. We recommend 800 points for 15mm singles tournament games (650 points for 25mm) and 1000 points for 15mm doubles games.

The army lists specify which troops can be used in a particular army. No other troops can be used. The number of bases of each type in the army must conform to the specified minima and maxima. Troops that have restrictions on when they can be used cannot be used with troops with a conflicting restriction. For example, troops that can only be used "before 1150" cannot be used with troops that can only be used "from 1150". All special instructions applying to an army list must be adhered to. They also apply to allied contingents supplied by the army.

All armies must have a C-in-C and at least one other commander. No army can have more than 4 commanders in total, including C-in-C, sub-commanders and allied commanders.

All armies must have a supply camp. This is free unless fortified. A fortified camp can only be used if specified in the army list. Field fortifications and portable defences can only be used if specified in the army list.

Allied contingents can only be used if specified in the army list. Most allied contingents have their own allied contingent list, to which they must conform unless the main army's list specifies otherwise.

BATTLE GROUPS

All troops are organized into battle groups. Commanders, supply camps and field fortifications are not troops and are not assigned to battle groups. Portable defences are not troops, but are assigned to specific battle groups.

Battle groups must obey the following restrictions:

- The number of bases in a battle group must correspond to the range specified in the army list.
- Each battle group must initially comprise an even number of bases. The only exception to this rule is that battle groups whose army list specifies them as 2/3 of one type and 1/3 of another, can comprise 9 bases if this is within the battle group size range specified by the list.
- A battle group can only include troops from one line in a list, unless the list specifies a mixed formation by specifying fractions of the battle group to be of types from two lines. e.g. 2/3 spearmen, 1/3 archers.
- All troops in a battle group must be of the same quality and training. When a choice of quality or training is given in a list, this allows battle groups to differ from each other. It does not permit variety within a battle group.
- Unless specifically stated otherwise in an army list, all troops in a battle group must be of the same armour class. When a choice of armour class is given in a list, this allows battle groups to differ from each other. It does not permit variety within a battle group.

Commander

EXAMPLE LIST

Here is a section of an actual army list, which will help us to explain the basics and some special features. The list specifies the following items for each historical type included in the army:

- Troop Type – comprising Type, Armour, Quality and Training.

- Capabilities – comprising Shooting and Close Combat capabilities.
- Points cost per base.
- Minimum and maximum number of bases in each battle group.
- Minimum and maximum number of bases in the army.

Troop name		Troop Type				Capabilities		Points per base	Bases per BG	Total bases
		Type	Armour	Quality	Training	Shooting	Close Combat			
Berber or Andalusian cavalry		Light Horse	Unprotected	Average	Undrilled	Javelins	Light Spear	7	4–6	12–42
Lamtuna or Hintata spearmen	Only Almoravids or Almohades	Heavy Foot	Protected	Superior	Drilled	–	Offensive Spearmen	10	2/3 or all 8–12	0–18
				Average				8		
Supporting archers		Light Foot	Unprotected	Superior	Drilled	Bow	–	6	1/3 or 0	0–9
				Average				5		
Other Berber or Black spearmen		Heavy Foot	Protected	Average	Undrilled	–	Defensive Spearmen	6	2/3 or all 8–12	16–48
Supporting archers		Light Foot	Unprotected	Average	Undrilled	Bow	–	5	1/3 or 0	0–24
Separately deployed Berber or Black archers		Light Foot	Unprotected	Average	Undrilled	Bow	–	5	6–8	0–24
		Medium Foot	Unprotected	Average	Undrilled	Bow	–	5	6–8	
Arab cavalry	Only Almohades	Cavalry	Armoured	Average	Undrilled	–	Lancers, Swordsmen	12	4–6	0–12
			Protected					9		

(Total bases column also shows 8–32 spanning the separately deployed Berber or Black archers rows)

SPECIAL FEATURES:

- Berber or Andalusian cavalry must be organized in battle groups of either 4 or 6 bases. The army must include at least 12 bases of Berber or Andalusian cavalry and cannot include more than 42.

- Only Almoravid or Almohad armies can have Lamtuna or Hintata spearmen. These must be organized either in battle groups of 8, 10 or 12 bases of spearmen, or in mixed battle groups of 6 bases of spearmen and 3 bases of supporting archers or 8 bases of spearmen and 4 bases of supporting archers. Each battle group can be of Superior or Average quality, but all of the bases in a battle group must be of the same quality. The list specifies the different points costs. The army cannot include more than 18 bases of Lamtuna or Hintata spearmen, nor more than 9 bases of archers supporting them.

- Other Berber or Black spearmen must be organized either in battle groups of 8, 10 or 12 bases of spearmen, or in mixed battle groups of 6 bases of spearmen and 3 bases of supporting archers or 8 bases of spearmen and 4 bases of supporting archers. The army must include at least 16 bases of other Berber or Black spearmen and cannot include more than 48. It cannot include more than 24 bases of archers supporting other Berber or Black spearmen.

- Separately deployed Berber or Black archers can either be Light Foot or Medium Foot.

They must be organized in battle groups of either 6 or 8 bases. All the bases in a battle group must be the same. The army cannot include more than 24 bases of separately deployed Berber or Black archers.

- The total number of bases of archers supporting other Berber or Black spearmen and separately deployed Berber or Black archers must be at least 8 and cannot be more than 32.

- Only Almohad armies can have Arab cavalry. These must be organized in battle groups of either 4 or 6 bases. They can be Armoured or Protected, but all the bases in a battle group must be the same. The list specifies the different points costs. The army cannot include more than 12 bases of Arab cavalry.

Troop name		Troop Type				Capabilities		Points per base	Bases per BG	Total bases
		Type	Armour	Quality	Training	Shooting	Close Combat			
Knights and sergeants	Only before 1150	Knights	Armoured	Superior	Undrilled	–	Lancers, Swordsmen	20	4–6	6–32
	Only from 1150	Knights	Heavily Armoured	Superior	Undrilled	–	Lancers, Swordsmen	23	4–6	
Feudal spearmen		Heavy Foot	Protected	Average	Undrilled	–	Defensive Spearmen	6	6–8	0–24
Mercenary spearmen		Heavy Foot	Armoured	Average	Drilled	–	Defensive Spearmen	9	6–8	0–8
			Protected					7		
Communal militia spearmen		Heavy Foot	Protected	Poor	Drilled	–	Defensive Spearmen	5	6–8	0–24

The rightmost "Total bases" column also shows an 8–40 bracket spanning the spearmen rows.

SPECIAL FEATURES:

- Before 1150, knights and sergeants are graded as Armoured. From 1150 they are graded as Heavily Armoured. They must be organized in battle groups of either 4 or 6 bases. The army must include at least 6 bases of knights and sergeants and cannot include more than 32.

- Feudal spearmen must be organized in battle groups of either 6 or 8 bases. The army cannot include more than 24 bases of feudal spearmen.

- Mercenary spearmen must be organized in battle groups of either 6 or 8 bases. They can be Armoured or Protected, but all the bases in a battle group must be the same. The list specifies the different points costs. The army cannot include more than 8 bases of mercenary spearmen.

- Communal militia spearmen must be organized in battle groups of either 6 or 8 bases. The army cannot include more than 24 bases of communal militia spearmen.

- The army must include at least 8 bases of feudal, mercenary or communal militia spearmen. It cannot include more than 40 bases total of feudal, mercenary and communal militia spearmen.

APPENDIX 2 – THEMED TOURNAMENTS

A tournament based on the "Feudal Europe" theme can include any of the armies listed in this book.

It can also include the following armies from our other army list books. These can only use options permitted between 1041 AD and 1300 AD:

DECLINE AND FALL

Lombard

Nikephorian Byzantine

WOLVES FROM THE SEA

Early Welsh

Viking

Norse-Irish

Norman

Anglo-Danish

SWORDS AND SCIMITARS

Komnenan Byzantine

INDEX

INDEX